‘As I was among the captives’

Joseph Campbell’s Prison Diary, 1922–1923

IRISH NARRATIVES

IRISH NARRATIVES

Series edited by David Fitzpatrick

Personal narratives of past lives are essential for understanding any field of history. They provide unrivalled insight into the day-to-day consequences of political, social, economic or cultural relationships. Memoirs, diaries and personal letters, whether by public figures or obscure witnesses of historical events, will often captivate the general reader as well as engrossing the specialist. Yet the vast majority of such narratives are preserved only among the manuscripts or rarities in libraries and archives scattered over the globe. The aim of this series of brief yet scholarly editions is to make available a wide range of narratives concerning Ireland and the Irish over the last four centuries. All documents, or sets of documents, are edited and introduced by specialist scholars, who guide the reader through the world in which the text was created. The chosen texts are faithfully transcribed, the biographical and local background explored, and the documents set in historical context. This series will prove invaluable for university and school teachers, providing superb material for essays and textual analysis in class. Above all, it offers a novel opportunity for readers interested in Irish history to discover fresh and exciting sources of personal testimony.

Other titles in the series:

Andrew Bryson's Ordeal: An Epilogue to the 1798 Rebellion, edited by Michael Durey
Henry Stratford Persse's Letters from Galway to America, 1821–1832, edited by James L. Pethica and James C. Roy
A Redemptorist Missionary in Ireland, 1851–1854: Memoirs by Joseph Prost, C.Ss.R. translated and edited by Emmet Larkin and Herman Freudenberger
Frank Henderson's Easter Rising: Recollections of a Dublin Volunteer, edited by Michael Hopkinson
A Patriot Priest: The Life of Father James Coigly, 1761–1798, edited by Dáire Keogh
'My Darling Danny': Letters from Mary O'Connell to Her Son Daniel, 1830–1832, edited by Erin I. Bishop
The Rebel in his Family: Selected Papers of William Smith O'Brien, edited by Richard and Marianne Davis
The Reynolds Letters: An Irish Emigrant Family in Late Victorian Manchester, edited by Lawrence W. McBride
A Policeman's Ireland: Recollections of Samuel Waters, RIC, edited by Stephen Ball
'The Misfit Soldier': Edward Casey's War Story, 1914–1918, edited by Joanna Bourke
Alfred Webb: The Autobiography of a Quaker Nationalist, edited by Marie-Louise Legg
Pádraig Ó Fathaigh's War of Independence: Recollections of a Galway Gaelic Leaguer, edited by Timothy G. McMahon
An Englishwoman in Belfast: Rosamond Stephen's Record of the Great War, edited by Oonagh Walsh

Forthcoming titles:

A Viceroy's Vindication: Sir Henry Sidney's Memoir of 1583, edited by Ciaran Brady
Loyalism and Labour in Belfast: The Autobiography of Robert McElborough, 1884–1952, edited by Emmet O'Connor and Trevor Parkhill

David Fitzpatrick teaches history at Trinity College, Dublin. His books include *Politics and Irish Life, 1913–1921* (1977, reissued 1998), *Oceans of Consolation: Personal Accounts of Irish Migration to Australia* (1995) and *The Two Irelands, 1912–1939* (1998).

‘As I was among the captives’
Joseph Campbell’s Prison Diary, 1922–1923

Edited by
Eiléan Ní Chuilleanáin

First published in 2001 by
Cork University Press
Cork
Ireland

© Cork University Press 2001

All rights reserved. No part of this book may be reprinted or reproduced or utilised by any electronic, mechanical or other means, now known or hereafter invented, including photocopying or recording or otherwise, without either the prior written permission of the Publishers or a licence permitting restricted copying in Ireland issued by the Irish Copyright Licensing Agency Ltd, The Irish Writers' Centre, 19 Parnell Square, Dublin 1.

British Library Cataloguing in Publication Data
A CIP catalogue record for this book is available from the British Library.
ISBN 1 85918 271 2

Typesetting by Red Barn Publishing, Skeagh, Skibbereen, Co. Cork
Printed in Ireland by ColourBooks, Baldoyle, Co. Dublin

Contents

Acknowledgements

I am grateful to Simon Campbell for permitting this edition of his father's Diary and to David Fitzpatrick and the late Flann Campbell for encouraging my return to the task of preparing an edition after a long interval. David Fitzpatrick deserves my gratitude as a determined and helpful editor. I am grateful also for the help given by Bernard Meehan and the staff of the Manuscripts Room at Trinity College, Dublin, and for suggestions by Nicholas Allen. I wish to thank Diane Sadler for her work in putting my original transcription on disc.

Introduction

The prison journal of the poet Joseph Campbell, now published in a representative selection for the first time, has a double interest, as an historical document from a critical time in Irish history, and as a literary work composed by a writer of great gifts and of high reputation in his day. Campbell's place among the poets of the Irish Revival is assured. Readers of this journal from the years 1922–3 will find that as well as a poet's talents he possessed the ability to write, in fluent prose, a lively, piercing and often humorous account of a lived experience. Apart from the direct pleasure of reading, his ideas and historical reflections are of great interest to anyone who wants to understand the ethos of that period in Irish history—one which was so critical for the country's development but whose outlook can now begin to appear strange and remote.

Campbell was already a well-known literary figure at the time of his imprisonment and the writing of the diary. He was born in 1879 in Belfast, but spent memorable periods of his childhood in the countryside on the borders of Down, Armagh and Louth from which his father William Henry Campbell came and where his grandfather still lived.[1] It was an escape from the commercial Anglophone modernity of Belfast, to a place connected to both the Gaelic past and the European Catholic world abroad. Irish was still spoken by old people (William Campbell had been beaten at school for speaking it as a child) and a great-uncle had been rector of the Irish College at Salamanca.[2]

William Campbell was a successful builder in Belfast, and Joseph was apprenticed to this trade in 1895 but left it after some sort of nervous collapse. His recovery took some years and as he got better he discovered that he was living in a new era of cultural activity. In 1898 two Northern poets, his cousin Ethna Carbery and her friend Alice Milligan, founded a periodical, *The Shan Van Vocht*. Its name, from the ballad celebrating the rebellion of a hundred years earlier, combined the historical reference with the poetic metaphor of Ireland personified as an old woman just as Yeats's *Cathleen Ni Houlihan* was to do in 1902. It was a milieu of commemoration and rediscovery, where Campbell was to encounter the Irish language revival via classes with the Gaelic League, and to discover Irish music and folklore and the writers to whom they were an inspiration (he met Padraic Colum at the Feis of the Nine Glens in County Antrim, in 1902). He found his way to the Ulster Literary Theatre, along with his sister Josephine who was to marry the playwright Sam Waddell; Waddell's Presbyterian background and the mixed marriage remind us that the literary world of Belfast included Protestants as well as Catholics.

By 1904 he had written the enduringly popular ballad, 'My Lagan Love', to a folk-tune collected by Herbert Hughes. This was the most successful of his early poems. In *The Rushlight*, published in 1906, there are vigorous experiments with folk-themes, with dramatic voice and with location; the title poem asserts that

> The very inner heart of it
> Of human travailing is knit;
> Its blood my blood, its bone my bone [3]

– and indeed there is an interest in human society and human variety throughout Campbell's poetry, combined as here with a self-assertion and a claim to speak for the many and for the Gaelic past. There are moments in his mature work when this bardic voice speaks with considerable authority; Austin Clarke picked out the lines from *The Mountainy Singer* of 1909:

> The silence of unlaboured fields
> Lies like a judgment on the air [4]

observing, 'he sums up an entire economic system in a phrase'. And Clarke writes illuminatingly about the sources of much of his work on folk themes:

> alone among these writers he drew inspiration ... not only from Irish sources but from the Gaelic tradition of the

> Highlands. No doubt this was due to his Northern ancestry. [. . .] We feel that such a legendary figure as the Gilly of Christ belongs to the entire Gaelic world. We feel that this mysterious messenger might appear one day in Cantyre or Skye and the next in Glen Columcille.[5]

The Gaelic imagery and rural mysticism of his poems appealed strongly to Irish readers and in time were also to make him an international reputation. A later volume, *Irishry* (1913), is full of sharp, satirical portraits which were perhaps less attractive to contemporary poetry-lovers, but it may be worth pointing out that there is a harsh, often comic note in much of the Irish verse of that decade, in the poems of Tom Kettle and Susan Mitchell but also in many of the poems in Yeats's volume, *Responsibilities* (London, 1914).

Campbell had moved from Dublin to London in 1906. This did not break his contact with Irish cultural and learned bodies—he was secretary to the Irish Literary Society and worked with Eleanor Hull at the Irish Texts Society, which was engaged in publishing the classic texts of earlier Gaelic literature. However, he made other contacts as well. He married Nancy Maude, a young woman with Anglo-Irish Unionist connections, in 1911; reference to Ezra Pound in the prison diary can be explained by the fact that Nancy had been at school with Dorothy Shakespeare, Pound's wife.

Joseph and Nancy returned to Ireland in 1912, settling first at Glencullen House, Co. Dublin. The move brought him into immediate contact with the new cultural and political institutions on their home ground. A play, *Judgment*, was performed at the Abbey, *Irishry* was published and the poet found himself being drawn into political activity. His return to Ireland coincided with the political crisis precipitated by the British Government's unwillingness to grant Home Rule to Ireland. The setting-up of an Irish Parliament had been conceded in theory, but was being delayed because of resistance by Unionists in the North-East. The foundation and arming of the Ulster Volunteers, pledged to resist Home Rule, was connived at by the British Government; it was followed in 1913 by the founding of the Irish Volunteers in Dublin, in support of the Home Rule movement. When war between Britain and Germany broke out in 1914, the Irish Volunteers split into those who supported the British war effort and those who continued to prepare for armed confrontation with Britain. Meanwhile, Home Rule was postponed until the return of peace. But, before the Armistice came, much in Ireland had been changed by the Rising of Easter 1916.

Campbell was involved from the beginning. He declares that he was present at the preliminary founding meeting of the Irish Volunteers. Later, the Citizen Army (James Connolly's socialist militia) drilled on the lawn of Glencullen House. After the Rising of 1916 he helped to organise the alternative civil regime which owed allegiance to Dáil Éireann with its courts and tax collection system. He worked on the organisation of several Sinn Féin election campaigns in the years 1917–19. In 1918–20 he was a member of the Republican District Court for East Wicklow, as well as Vice-Chairman of Wicklow Co. Council in the enforced absence of the chairman Robert Barton, who was in an English prison.[6] In 1921 he and his wife and three young sons moved to Lackandarragh, near Enniskerry, Co. Wicklow.

In July 1921 a Truce was declared and negotiations began between Dáil Éireann and the British Government. The previous year, the Government of Ireland Act had created a separate state with its own parliament in the six 'Protestant counties' of north-east Ulster. Now the rest of Ireland was offered a limited independence, i.e. 'Dominion status' with a parliament whose members would take an Oath of Allegiance to the King. Campbell's reverence for the leaders of the Rising led to a refusal to see their Republican ideals compromised in the Anglo-Irish Treaty of 1921. Like de Valera and Countess Markievicz, like many of those who had led the battle against the Black-and-Tans, he regarded the signing of the Treaty (with its acceptance of Partition and thus abandonment of the Northern nationalists among whom he had grown up) as a betrayal, and was willing to take up arms against the new Provisional Government of the Irish Free State. His nationalism, like that of many of his colleagues, was lofty, poetic, with a cult of heroism and a faith in the destiny of the Gael which has been seen as proto-fascist, but was often combined with a respect for democracy and a dislike for dictators. In his diary he recorded his admiration for Garibaldi but commented ironically on the pretensions of Mussolini.

Most of those who supported the Treaty and formed the Provisional Government had also fought in the war against Britain. They had accepted the Treaty because of the threat of a renewal of that war, which they felt they had not the resources to win. Ironically, they were now faced with another war against their former comrades, in which weapons had to be borrowed from the departing British occupying force. The stage was set for tragedy, for fraternal conflict and killing, though many friendships survived.

An uneasy peace marked the early months of 1922. Republicans occupied the Four Courts and other buildings in Dublin in April; for a time nothing was done to dislodge them. Then, at the insistence of Britain, the Free State attacked using borrowed artillery. Those inside surrendered on 30 June. Wicklow IRA units who had been coming to their relief attempted to fight on but were dispersed. Campbell's diary refers very briefly to events in North Wicklow which must have taken place about this time and in which he was concerned—the burning of the barracks at 'E–' (Enniskerry), a night out 'with the tree fellers' (making roadblocks on the Dublin to Enniskerry Road) at 'the Scalp', and his arrest in the street in Bray on 7 July. He had gone there, according to the account he was to write in 1942, cycling on the back roads, to arrange for wounded Republican fighters to be treated in a hospital.[7]

The next few weeks were chaotic and stressful in the extreme. After a week in Bray he was transferred to Wellington Barracks (later Griffith Barracks) in Dublin; the convoy was ambushed on the road to Dublin by Republicans, who mistook them, according to the 1942 account, for Free State recruits. Two weeks later he was moved to Mountjoy Prison where he was to stay until the following February. A large number of prisoners, including Campbell, were then removed to the Curragh where army camps, 'Tintowns' recently vacated by the British, were turned into internment camps. There they remained for the rest of the year 1923, some of them well into 1924. Campbell was released in December 1923.

Life in prison was far from peaceful. Prisoners were being held without trial subject to the arbitrary decisions of a Government whose legitimacy was being daily attacked. In Mountjoy there was discomfort and privation: the prison was overcrowded, rations were inadequate and food parcels from outside were stopped more than once. There were terrifying occurrences, from occasional sniping to an outright gun-battle within the jail, as well as the horror of the execution without trial of four prominent members of the Four Courts garrison as a reprisal by the Free State for the Republicans' assassination of a TD. Things were calmer in the Curragh, but there was still an atmosphere of danger, for example after an escape tunnel was discovered in April. Rumours of the conditions in the 'Glasshouse' where rule-breakers were sent were terrifying.

News from the outside world could raise spirits or dash them. In April the death of Liam Lynch, who had been leading Republican resistance in the South, was desolating news. It was followed by a Republican ceasefire which raised the prisoners' hopes of release. There was a General Election in August, news of which was eagerly followed. The murder of Noel Lemass, whose body was found on 12 October on the Dublin mountains following his capture by Free State forces in July, aroused public feeling and shocked the prisoners. At certain times they felt they were part of a wider struggle; at others it seemed as if the rest of Ireland had forgotten them. In October, Republicans in all jails and camps went on hunger-strike in a bid to capture public attention and force the Government to release them unconditionally, but the strike was called off in November without having achieved anything.

Campbell's diary records these events and many more. It was formally begun in Mountjoy but incorporates notes of the weeks before he arrived there. From very early on, perhaps from the first moment of its existence, it was intended for publication; thus it was not only a record of the historic experiences the writer was having but a fully-worked piece of literary art, a testimony of his fidelity to his mission as a writer.

He was inspired by the idea of emulating great prisoners: the Old Testament prophet Ezekiel (a possible title mentioned early on was 'As I was among the Captives' from *Ezekiel 1, 1*), Sir Walter Raleigh, John Bunyan, even Leigh Hunt. An Irish classic of the prison genre was John Mitchel's *Jail Journal*. (Campbell had never read Mitchel, though he notes that Ó Neachtáin's Irish translation was in the camp.) Perhaps more importantly, for a writer who had many contacts with modernist as well as traditional writing, he compares himself to Joyce, who recorded the minute details of his own and others' lives, and to Proust, who had chronicled his society though shut away by illness as the prisoners were by barbed wire.

The unsettled life in Mountjoy was hardly conducive to writing regularly, and at first the reader gathers what is happening or has happened by implication rather than being told. Gaps have to be filled in. A few words and phrases are recalled from an incident such as his arrival at Mountjoy with empty pockets at the end of July 1922. Major events such as the death of Arthur Griffith on 12 August of a stroke, and the death in an ambush of Michael Collins on 22 August—the latter an event which made a deep impression on many Republicans—are mentioned only obliquely. By November, the reader can trace the record of a sequence of events: from the executions of four rank-and-file Republicans on 17 November to that of Childers on 24 November, from the assassination of Seán Hales on 7 December to the reprisal execution on the 8th of O'Connor, Mellows, Barrett and McKelvey.

Campbell's own response is always part of the story. As self-preoccupied as Stephen Dedalus, he lets the reader know how the shock of his comrades' deaths affects his religious faith. But, sharp-eyed as Leopold Bloom, he records details such as the demeanour of the priest and doctor who had officiated at the execution. The Joycean tone of some of the observations may be fortuitous; he may be simply reminding himself to write up at a later stage something he has just spotted, such as (in a marginal note to an entry written in the Curragh: on 11 July 1923, 'CONNEMARA MAN picking Crabs from Balls.') But the greater part of the diary is written in a fluid, spiky style, full of verbal originality: coinages like 'arsey' to describe someone's walk, American slang, Gaelicisms like 'angashore', and always the use of colour and precise detail. It is a style well suited to describe events as they happen, whether in the clipped minute-by-minute account of the searches in April 1923 which led to the discovery of the attempted escape-tunnel, or the combination of relief and dejection in the reported speech on the November day that saw the end of the hunger-strike. Occasionally, as in the account (9 August 1923) of an incident involving the mad prisoner 'Siki', he writes with a more deliberate, explanatory style with longer sentences—I suspect this passage was rewritten from notes made at the time and may have been intended for publication on its own.

Campbell sees himself in part as the observant recorder who speaks for his comrades and preserves and vindicates their experience for posterity. But at many points he is at odds with the half-educated, generally quite young men with whom he finds himself confined. He and his wife Nancy (English-born but as fiercely Republican as he at this stage of their lives) had moved in literary and political circles in London and continued to do so in Dublin (as is illustrated by the extract from Nancy's letter to Joseph quoted on 4 November 1922). His international reputation is suggested by the fact that his poem 'The Hills of Cualann', translated into German via 'a German poet in New York', appeared in *Jugend*, June 1922, and reached him in Mountjoy. W. B. Yeats, who had just been given the Nobel Prize, was said to be lobbying for his release at the end of 1923. Campbell was a man who had lived and travelled much more, and achieved more international recognition, than his companions in prison, and he often feels superior to them. His close associates are two other intellectuals, the very young, talented and well-connected Francis Stuart and the Gaelic scholar Seán a' Chóta (Seán Kavanagh). It is interesting to see that while Campbell's superiority seems to have been generally accepted—other prisoners call him 'sir' and 'Mr Campbell'—Kavanagh's was resisted. But he was the camp 'fixer', able to organise newspapers and the posting of clandestine letters.

With Stuart and Kavanagh especially, Campbell expresses his discontent and his criticisms of the Ireland that is emerging from the struggle, and discusses literary projects. He comments, on 8 June 1923, on 'the humbug of W. B. Yeats. The mockery of his Cathleen ni Houlihan & the poem in Responsibilities about the poet with the sword upstairs', and refers to 'My intended attack in the poem: "The blindness of the Bards", which I meditated in Mountjoy'. The diary itself is discussed by the three literary men: both its historic significance and the physical problems of writing and concealing it. There are moments of panic during the repeated searches; once, he reports: 'A packet of my journal was on me, tucked between the blankets, newspaper cuttings, list of names for unemployment schemes etc. Wasn't disturbed, praises be', on 7 August 1923—and on 24 August: 'Transferred packet to O/C hut . . . Hurley by name. A friend of Seán's—a fine, big honest looking fellow. He came out of hut with a copy of *Fuinn na Smól [Songs of the Thrushes]* open in his hand & took the packet eagerly.'

The anxiety is not merely because the author might be victimised by the authorities for keeping a secret journal. Because of its outspokenness about his opinions of his own colleagues, Campbell's diary could have been a notable propaganda own-goal if it had been captured. The soldier who smuggled post in and out was well aware that, though the shooting war was over, the propaganda war which had been an even more important part of the battle for Ireland was still going on—indeed, in a sense, it went on being waged for another seventy years. Seán a' Chóta reported to Campbell about the risky system:

> [28 August 1923] Seán Kavanagh in after breakfast. Whispered in my ear as I sat on bed-edge: *'Tá siad scaoilte chun siubhal'* ['They're on their way']. 'What' said I. 'The letters are gone per Ham & Eggs[8]. "I'm your dish, said he if you don't send anything that will get into the papers."' My letters put into Nurse Cahill's envelope to be reposted from Dunleary. Norah's ring gone.

The ring was for an Englishwoman with whom Campbell was conducting an affair by correspondence from jail. One reason why Kavanagh's company appealed to him was probably that it gave him a chance to discuss what he refers to at one stage as 'the poet's privilege' of illicit sexual relations. Many accounts of the generation that made the Irish revolution stress the men's sexual innocence. C. S. Andrews in his autobiography written in the 1970s attributes this to their education by the Christian Brothers; he comments on the rarity of affairs between male volunteers and the women from the female branch of the movement, Cumann na mBan. He asserts that while swearing was rife, 'Dirty talk was rare and homosexuality non-existent.'[9] The prisoners lived at very close quarters; the mass of them were young, even the leaders—Michael Collins was thirty-one at his death, Liam Lynch under thirty. Imprisonment seems to have led to an accentuation of that sexual repression which was, in any case, the lot of this generation of better-educated Irishmen who would have had to postpone marriage until they had worked for several years and perhaps paid for the education of younger members of their families.

Campbell too comments on the innocence of many of his fellow-prisoners. Kavanagh, who came from a less repressed society in the Gaeltacht, was corresponding with a number of women and talked more freely about sex; Campbell, on 11 July 1923, records how he 'told me stories of his early puberty. The tall woman of Dunquin at turf-rick up in the bog. She 45, he 15.' As the prisoners allowed themselves to think about the possibility of release, however, sex was openly discussed by the older ones though the more puritanical objected:

> [2 December 1923] Biscuit very ribald. Protest by Tommy Campbell: 'I thought you were a follower of Padraic Pearse, Cary.' Married men—'the spring bed will rock when we get out.' 'You'd want a week's feeding first.' 'I'd tackle it this minute if I got out.'

Campbell's experience when he was released was less cheerful than his comrades' blithe speculation. His wife had taken in a young Dublin

Republican who helped her on the farm. Although he left when her husband was released, the relationship between her and the young man contributed to the break-up of the marriage in August of 1924. A year later Campbell went to America, where he may well be said to have invented 'Irish Studies' by founding a School of Irish Studies attached to Fordham University in New York. The School lasted from 1926 to 1932 when it was amalgamated into the Fordham English Department. Campbell remained in New York making a living as a writer until 1939, when he returned to Ireland. He went back to Lackandarragh, and managed, barely, to survive by writing and broadcasting. In June 1944 neighbours noticed that his post had not been collected and found him dead on the hearth of his cottage.

Imprisonment had changed his life. For younger men it was an episode in their education and in the history of their country to which they looked back with pride or scepticism depending on their view of what they had achieved. Campbell's internment in his forties, as a member of a defeated army, had led to the loss of his home and to a disaffection which can be seen developing in the Diary. From one who had been in the thick of Ireland's political and literary life he had become an outsider and presently an exile.

The Prison Diary went with him to the United States. He did not publish it in his lifetime, perhaps because of the outspokenness of the comments on many named individuals. When he was returning to Ireland in 1939 he left all his papers, including the diary and many letters of the early 1920s, with an Irish-American woman, Mairéad MacCartney. In 1963 my mother, the novelist Eilís Dillon, stayed with Mrs MacCartney in New York and was asked to take charge of the papers—probably because of her Republican credentials (she was a niece of Joseph Plunkett, executed in 1916; her surviving uncles had spent long periods in prison in the 1920s, 1930s and 1940s; my father too had been interned in the Curragh as a young man of twenty). She accepted this charge although she herself was about to move from Ireland to Rome; she expected that, since I was academically inclined, I would in due course take on the job of sorting and editing.

Many things have made that job a slow one. My academic interest in what was then known as Anglo-Irish literature was, and remains, limited. The mass of the papers are of interest to a biographer of Campbell or a cultural historian rather than a literary scholar. When I became friendly with Joseph Campbell's son Flann and his wife Mary, and met his other son Simon, it became possible to arrange that the papers I held should be deposited with theirs in the Library of Trinity College, Dublin.

The prison diary had always seemed to me an interesting and attractive text that ought to be published, and in the 1970s I made a typewritten transcript and tried to interest a number of publishers, including the late Liam Miller, in bringing out an edition of it. Miller and another publisher found it too long, and suggested I make a selection, but neither could give me a firm commitment to publication. The Irish Writers' Co-Operative planned to bring it out in an abridged edition, but ceased trading just as I was to start work on a final text. I decided that I would spend no more time on the project until there was an interested publisher who had some chance of staying in business for long enough to bring out a book. I used some research funds that came my way to have the text copied on a disc in case that time ever came. The 'Irish Narratives' series provided me with the opportunity, for which I am very grateful to David Fitzpatrick and Cork University Press, to bring this lengthy process to a conclusion.

Campbell's diary is filed in the Manuscripts Department, TCD, as MSS 10173–10176. It is written partly on loose sheets, partly in notebooks which are worn and frayed at the edges. Some of the loose sheets may have originally been pages of a similar notebook. The early entries especially are scraps. The two letters to Nancy Campbell which open the diary are written on small leaves of a notepad; they are presumably copies of letters which may or may not have been actually sent. The diary does contain other copies of letters which were sent.

The entries are not always in chronological order. In early December 1922 Campbell reminisces about his transfer from Wellington Barracks in late July (notes of the main dates in his own imprisonment are jotted down several times) and announces a plan to 'celebrate the heroism of my contemporaries', dating the entry in July, before returning to jot down ribald expressions of other prisoners and the urgent events of the day. Tintown entries are occasionally made several times a day, sometimes incorporating notes which seem to have been scribbled on the spot, for example the entries for 23 April 1923.

The notebooks seem also to have served as scrapbooks—there are many extracts from books and newspapers which Campbell was reading at the time, most of which I have omitted. The last letters of Mellows and Dick Barrett, on 8 December 1922, are copied in, as is the last message to fellow-prisoners from Dr Fearon TD (with a note: 'Copy given to me by Liam Barrett, Hut 5, of Cork') on 23 July 1923.

As Campbell, once prison life had settled down, wrote almost every day unless he was ill, the diary is both long and repetitive. To reflect the general publishing format of this series, it was resolved to reduce the almost 190,000 words to 35,000 and to preserve the integrity of the individual entries. This has resulted in the sacrifice of much interesting material and the making of some difficult decisions. It seemed worthwhile, for example, to keep the whole day-by-day account of the hunger-strike. But there is almost nothing in this edition on the Irish class run by Seán Kavanagh, nothing of the lighter material such as the Camp Sports in the summer of 1923, few of the entries describing the excitement surrounding releases. Several accounts of interesting conversations are omitted, such as Campbell's talk, on 9 August 1923, with a Dundalk prisoner, where he reminisces about the time spent in that area as a child in the company of the uncle who was parish priest of Annaverna: 'I told him of the romance Annaverna was to me as a child—a Gaelic-speaking village up in the mountains.' In the conversation and in Campbell's reminiscences, the lost South Ulster Gaeltacht is referred to as still existing in the speech of old people in Omeath, and the paradox of a Belfast poet identifying with Gaelic culture is softened.

Some of the reported conversations comment on the political situation in ways that show how Campbell felt his Ulster identity: [9 December 1923] 'Harbinson speaks as if only Tyrone & Fermanagh mattered to Ireland. But what of Antrim, Down, Armagh, Derry. I am an Irishman & I was born in Co. Down.' And on 12 November, reporting a dialogue with Seán Kavanagh: '"There's no Ireland, Ireland is a thing of the past, There won't be any Ireland for years to come. Six counties—twenty six counties, agh! She's no better than she was in the days of Spenser or Sir Walter Raleigh." "A trembling sod, as the Four Masters said."'

Some of the entries I have left out contain illuminating comments on noted characters such as, again on 12 November 1923, Harry Boland's brother Gerry: 'Watkins spoke of Gerry Boland's character—"wouldn't kill a rabbit"—a vegetarian—unlike his brother Harry or the other brother—the "hard root" from America—a real Yank. One day during a scrap a crowd from Rathfarnham—looters & comandeerers—took out an old horse & dray. Loose shoe—bleeding fetlock—all red & raw. Gerry nearly plugged the fellow for it. That was his way—terribly hot & determined."'

Other entries comment on the daily activities, including craftwork, which the prisoners engaged in. There are revealing observations on religious life and one or two suggest the demoralisation of the prisoners. The chapel was pilfered for things that might be of use, and on 12 November 1923 a prisoner observes that it is 'an old kip'. He goes on: 'In the Kinlar[10] there was a proper chapel (equipped by British), with stations of cross, & you'd see a fellow in there saying his prayers like you would in a chapel in the city.' The combination of irreverence and religious nostalgia is striking. When the silver spoon used at Mass goes missing on 22 September 1923, a prisoner is sent to look for it. He finds it but keeps it for himself and an onlooker comments, 'It's beaten into a Tara brooch now'. The prisoners' crafts thus appear not simply as occupational therapy but as expressing a cultural identity at odds with that offered by the Catholic church.

In the text, some names are initials and dashes, others blacked out. The blacking-out may possibly have been done at some stage when the diary was being smuggled out of Tintown in order to minimise the scandal if it were captured. This would hardly have been very effective though, since it is not hard, even at this distance, to fill in a number of the gaps. I have attempted to identify individuals and events as far as possible in the notes. In making these identifications I have found Michael Hopkinson's *Green against Green: The Irish Civil War* (Dublin, 1988), Padraic O'Farrell's *Who's Who in the Irish War of Independence and the Civil War* (Dublin, 1997) and the notes to J. A. Gaughan (ed.), *Memoirs of Senator Joseph Connolly* (Dublin, 1996) especially useful. Dorothy Macardle's *The Irish Republic* (London, 1937) is a very full if partisan account.

Many autobiographical accounts of the period 1916–23 in Ireland survive. The 'classic' is Ernie O'Malley's *On Another Man's Wound* (London, 1936) which describes the War of Independence in terms of a young man's coming to consciousness in a critical time for his society. The experience of hunger-strike is described in *Days of Fear* (London, 1928) by Frank Gallagher, who attempts to convey the emotional horror of the experience, and in drier language by Peadar O'Donnell in *The Gates Flew Open* (London, 1932). C. S. Andrews's *Dublin Made Me* (Dublin, 1979) has the attraction of being written by a man for whom the war was a prelude to an active career as a public servant. Andrews looks back over a lifetime and can see the changes in society as a whole, not merely in its political superstructure. For Andrews and O'Malley, both active men, imprisonment appears as something to be endured stoically as a forced interruption of action. But Campbell is a contemplative, for whom the internment camp is a chance to observe humanity in its essence.

Editorial Note

The passages printed here are all complete entries from Campbell's diary, starting with a date (or occasionally a time). When he made several entries on the same day (as he did, for example, on 8 December 1922) I have not always reproduced all the entries. I have not reproduced his variations in writing dates, which include the forms '8/12/22', '8:XII:22' and '8th Dec. '22' among others. I have expanded the names of individuals from initials where possible, but in places I have allowed initials which are very frequently used to stand, e.g. S. K. for Seán Kavanagh.

Joseph Campbell

Prison Diary
1922–23

Manuscripts Department, TCD MSS 10173–10176

[Campbell began to plan his diary very early in his imprisonment. He kept notes on scraps of paper and also preserved copies of letters he wrote. His arrest and his time as a prisoner at Bray are recounted in copies, which he kept, of two letters to his wife Nancy Campbell who, with their three sons, Simon, Gilly and Flann, continued to live on the farm at Lackandarragh, Co. Wicklow during his imprisonment.]

[1]

Thursday 6 June 1922

I am a prisoner in the Royal Hotel, Main St., Bray. Arrested by Free State Army on information of an ex-soldier in street. Rotten accommodation and no food so far. The O.C. is a grocer's assistant in Clery's shop in Main St. Treats me like a dog. No charge formulated yet. I am one of six other prisoners—one of them Frank Crowley of Shankhill. Up the Republic!

Joseph

[2]

Bray Wednesday 12 noon.

Things are pretty rotten and disorganised here. Nine extra prisoners in, and neither the food nor the sleeping accommodation is as good as at the beginning. I slept last night in my clothes, with not a stitch to cover me except my pyjamas which I wrapped round my feet to keep warm. We got orders to be ready to start at 6 a.m. this morning for (1st.) Wellington Bks (2nd) then Portobello (3rd) then the Naval Base, Dunleary, but so far nothing has happened. The Free State raiding parties are now carrying hostages in their cars as a protection against ambush. It is 12 noon now & we are still hanging around waiting for orders. The rooms are unswept, "thrones" spilled over the floors by visitors, beds unmade etc owing to the uncertainty as to whether we go or stay the night. Up to this we have kept the prisoners' quarters spick & span—I am Commdt!—but as I say, all is disorganised today.

Snipers (F. S.) occupy the windows of our rooms these last few nights, & it is an eerie sensation to go to sleep with the expectation that you may be shot at any moment. The garrison is the lowest of the low, without moral scruple & if they act without orders God help us!! I hear such a lot of violent talk among them in the lavatory!!! while sitting concealed in the W.C. Whether I get syphilis from the dirty basins or not is in God's hands. Half the men are rotten with it. If only we knew where we were to go & stay permanently until we escaped or were released we would be content; but a night at Dunleary, another elsewhere—with ambushing parties lying in wait everywhere—doesn't conduce to the settled life. It's a great, if disagreeable, experience. Ask intelligent, not-to-be-put-down people to visit the prisoners regularly. If publicity is not given nasty things may happen—especially in these barracks liable to attack.

I have already lost my razor-strop & comb—"pinched" by the ex-Tommies who have free access to our rooms while we are at exercise. We are not allowed to lock the doors & there is no discipline as in a properly-run jail like Mountjoy. Two further Bray prisoners have arrived. They are being arrested hourly at their homes whither they have returned from the hills! I warn you that Lackandarragh may be raided & searched, so be prepared.

Up the Republic!

Ever

Joseph.

[The diary begins after Campbell's transfer to Mountjoy. It begins as scraps and, especially at first, includes several extracts copied from books. Most of these I am omitting. It is clear too that Campbell often "wrote up" later from notes made in haste on the spot. Scraps record sayings and incidents, such as the following entry, the first for Mountjoy:]

'I'm bitched, balloxed and bewildered'[1]

'He'd talk a hole through a pot.'

As black as the hob of hell.
P. Halley, Mountjoy.
31 July 22

The incident in the prison yard when the guard levelled his rifle and shot a grey-blue pigeon that had just alighted on the hospital chimney. The pigeon fluttered away, some of its wing feathers gone. I felt that he had fired at the spirit of Ireland.

2 September 1922

The girl prisoner waving to the men in the ring through the barred hospital window. She had been arrested after an ambush near Leixlip—Lucan on the previous evening & brought in at 10 p.m. Miss—F –, Blessington St. Dublin.

Sunday 10 September 1922

7 August 1922

The prisoners of the 1st Northern Division arrived in Mt.Joy at 1.30 a.m. after a voyage from Buncrana, Lough Swilly to the North Wall. They brought into the fetid air of the compound something of the salt tang of the sea & of the heather & water about Glenveagh Castle where they were arrested. Inch Fort—rheumatism caught from sleeping on the stone floors of the dungeons.

The sound of Miss MacLeod's reel heard from a fiddle being played in Cell 3, A2 landing (Tommy Duke's cell.)

2 September 1922

Ribbed glass in panes except two which were 'plain' & which allowed us to see the moon. Convicts never see the moon.

16 September 1922

We were talking in Cell 9—about the situation in Ireland when suddenly P.J. Ryan rose up & said 'Oh, the moon.' We all rose up &

saw the full harvest moon through the bars of the cell window. On the cell wall, to the left, I saw the shadow of the bars. You have no idea what the moon meant to us. Oscar Wilde & the sky etc. etc. (The Hunter's Moon)

Lincoln: 'When I can get a chance to hit that thing I will hit it hard.' The gang of 4 prisoners—one lifer—two three years—one fifteen years, an Italian, who drew a knife & stabbed a man fatally—a little, broad shouldered, lemon-faced, stubborn man. Outside the ring, where the Republican prisoners were foregathered, carting away gravel in a handcart. Beside them stood a tall, fair warder in the blue uniform cap & brightly-shined silver buttons—a lower type than the men he watched. The blue handkerchief for belt—their own shabby clothes—the white armlet with 3 stripes etc. etc. 'Good day, comrade' said I to a bearded 'lag' who returned the greeting in a strong Munster accent.

20 September 1922

The wonderful picture made by the band at the dancing class in the prison compound. Tommy Duke's perennially interesting figure as the fiddler, his bow arm crooked, his hand leaning pathetically against his fiddle—all in black. The young drummer astride the stool beating a roll ('ruffle') on his drum. Tom McG—with the English concertina, his black-red face aglow with pleasure. The gentle melancholy of the banjo player. The flute-players trilling the quick passages of 'Miss McLeod's Reel'. The dull gas-flares partly illuminating the heads of the dancers & the loungers against the wall. Such a scene as Jack Yeats would have delighted in painting.

22 September 1922

There was (We had) an Irish hooley in the Wing—Dances—'The Siege of Ennis', 'The High Caul Cap', 'The Walls of Limerick,' 'The Bridge of Athlone,' a slip-jig from the Derryman, J– H–, songs etc. Had broken up after 'The Soldiers Song' sung at attention with full-throated effect etc. I was in No 3 cell when 'Bang! Bang!'—the concussion of the shots dingling our ears—from the guards outside. Then another shot & uproar in A3 landing & cries of 'O/C Wing!' 'O/C/Wing' 'Doctor! fetch the doctor.' A prisoner wounded. Then 'Back to your cells!' & after a time quiet. The guard passed up armed with the prison doctor. Then a drunken soldier (the man who had fired the fatal shot) was brought under escort through the central hall. Whispers from pyjamaed & nightshirted men peering from cells, 'Hit in the small of the back!' Then silence & sleep.

Sunday 10.45 p.m. 24 September 1922

1 October 1922

Sounds

How low, how insistent are the sounds of authority—the clink of the guard's keys, the click of the sentry's rifle as he withdraws the bolt, the fall of an ejected cartridge-case on the compound floor etc. One hears them all day & all hours of the day.—The jerk of the turned bolt in the wards of the gate lock. The steady march, up & down, of the prying guard in the silence of night. Little sounds, but signifying how much & how evil!

The other strident, tearing sounds of authority: The 'Lights out!' The 'Get back to your cells'—'you fucking bastards'; the concussion of the shot fired in compound or yard outside; the bullet ricocheting off the bar of the cell window, the splintering crash of glass, the cry of 'O/C Wing! O/C/Wing! Doctor!' from A3 Landing & then—the low sounds again, the pad, pad of the M. O. & Red Cross to the wounded man, the whisperings from white figures in the cell doors & then—primeval silence which in itself will be the ultimate Lord & Master of Authority. 1 October 1922

Six revolver shots fired in quick succession 4 October 22. Red cross men with bandages & styptics.

Blue tattoo mark scrawled across right arm of prisoner: 'Lily Woods, 1907.' On left arm 'All Wiped out—1909.' Seen on a lag in Portland.

R. B. [*Robert Barton*][2]

6 October 1922

Tattoo marks all over body. Even rings on penis.

6 October 1922

10 October 1922, Tuesday[3]

About 8-30 a.m. a heavy burst of revolver fire—then the Q. M.'s voice (Led–): 'Orderlies! Get back from gates. Back to your cells.' More firing; then running of feet along the compound floor. Several orderlies ran past cell door (No. 9) on A2 Landing. The Wings began to echo with concentrated revolver & rifle fire, the detonations making a headachy racket. Silence—which you could positively hear—about 9.15 a.m. 'The beating of the wings of death,' as I said to Dr. Ryan.[4] Firing began again. Voices from cell-doors: 'Waste it away! Churchill will give you more.' Intense rifle fire until 11 a.m. Banging of prisoners on cell doors, 'Give us our breakfast. We're hungry.' Like primitive animals. In the intervals of the rifle-fire could be heard the tap-tap-tap of an industrious ring-maker in a cell down the Wing. About 11 a.m. I ventured forth & got a can of water to make tea. Broken glass littered the floor below & plaster & limewash everywhere. Rumours afloat. Dead sentry's cap in hall A2 landing & pool of blood. 2 F. S. dead; 1 R.—P—B –[5] 9 or 10 wounded. About 9-30 a.m. in an interval between the rifle-shots the bell of Berkley St. church began to ring for Mass. How paradoxical it seemed! Dr. Ryan talking across to me from his mattress all the time. 'Reaction after crisis'—'Psychic vibrations'—'Second sight'—etc. etc. 'What a joy to be a Republican prisoner'.

10 October 1922

There has been an ominous calm all day after the battle in the morning, 8.30 a.m. to 11 a.m. Rumours that there are dead 3 F. S. and 1 R.—P—B—. First report that 9 were wounded, but it is now reduced to 1 R. The F. S. wounded not known. The sentry's cap lay in the pool of blood on A2 landing for quite a long time. The poor devil himself was not removed for quite 15 minutes after he was hit owing to intense fire. All the guard are white-faced, tense & generally 'windy'. No breakfast this morning except a cup of tea which we made over gas-jet in No. 9 cell. Not allowed out into exercise-ring all day. As darkness fell it was quite jumpy to be out on the landings at all. About 7-30 p.m. I went down to gas-jet at lavatory on A2 to boil some milk. R. B. [*Robert Barton*] and Dr. R—[*Ryan*] were in No 9 cell playing chess. Liam Mellows'[6] fiddle broken up. A shot suddenly rang out—rifle—which gave me a shiver down my backbone. It was fired at young Penrose who was crossing bridge near sentry's post (against orders). I wondered if I would be able to get back to my cell. Dodged along from door to door. When I got to 13 was quite relieved to think I was so near 'home'. As I got in R.B. & Dr. R. were on their feet. A mug of milk was spilled all over the cell floor. A prisoner passing along landing from top dashed in for cover as shot went off & capsised his supper. R.B. immediately left for his own cell. Firing all the night.

C. Wing prisoners kept out in Ring all day without food. Andy Cooney[7] arrested & taken to basement. C. Wing cells raided & property broken & stolen. Liam Mellows' fiddle broken up.

11 October 1922

All normal again, more or less. Exercise-yard open. Watched J. Begley, Scully, R. B.—& Dr. R—play auction bridge in 16 cell. S –D— came in about 5 p.m. with 'buckshee' tobacco from an unclaimed parcel. He distributed it around. Very grateful for smokes owing to parcel being stopped as punishment for the attack of yesterday morning. Still unsafe to be on landings after dark.

12 October 1922

This morning between 1 a.m. and 3 a.m. heard lorries arriving & shouting of men outside in yard. Then scuffles outside guard room in central-hall, shouting & 1 shot from revolver fired. 'Double to it!' from the guard & then scuffling of feet, running & suppressed screams. Prisoners maltreated as they arrived. Kicked, most likely on backside &

threatened with revolver butts. Just before dinner 11-30—12 noon we were sitting R.B., Dr. R—& myself in No—cell, chatting when in walks a tall F. S. policeman—P.A.[8]—in uniform with a drawn revolver in his right hand. He pushed open cell door without warning. Outside a rifleman at the ready, stood guard. 'P.A.' looked quickly round cell—at pictures on walls & behind door, & without saying a word walked out again. Sinister & menacing. Prisoners, white-faced & expectant at cell-doors (how they hug the doorposts since the shooting) discussing situation.

'Priests, you know, have a great temptation to alcoholism. The fact of drinking wine at the Mass before breakfast predisposes them to it. It's easy to get fond of wine under such circumstances. You heard of the rule, did you?, in the diocese of Achonry? The "post-prandial rule", as it was called. No priest in the diocese was allowed to drink any kind of spirituous liquor before dinner—usually 4 o'clock p.m. in the parochial houses. I heard of a priest living on the border of the next diocese boast that by taking a walk of a hundred yards he could get a drink before dinner without breaking the post-prandial rule in Achonry.'

Dr J. Ryan 13 October 1922

22–23 October 1922 Sun-Mon.

Was awakened suddenly out of my sleep in Cell 9, A2 by the sound of a woman's voice—like Nancy's—calling 'Joseph!!'. The voice cried only once and quite close as if under my cell window. My heart gave one or two jumps, for the voice sounded as if in distress. I pictured Nancy having climbed the outer prison wall & unseen by the guards, rushing across the main outer yard in a desperate effort to find me. This was during the time of suspense which followed the shooting of the 10th Oct. when letters & parcels were stopped, & no communication with the outer world was allowed. I fell over asleep again & forgot about the incident until the morning of the 23rd Oct.

Sat. 28 October 1922

Fine clear, airy, sunny October morning, with a bracing nip in the air. The clouds high, white—luminous, piled in a blue sky over barbed wire bars of the ring-rail in the exercise yard. The Fianna Boys drilling in the ring under Commdt. L–L–. The sense of freedom in the white, moving clouds beyond the bars of the ring, reflected in the boys' ready response to the commands. The promise of ultimate freedom in clouds & Fianna boys. Pools of water lying in the ring reflecting the bright, after-rain light. Sentry, armed with rifle, on duty.

Mountjoy—the grey stone dungeon-like fabric of the walls. The cell windows, with rags etc., whirligigs from the outside. The grey chimney-towers, with smoke belching forth. The ragged, faded Tricolour, shameful to be flown in such a cause—the flag of the poets & freemen Pearse, MacDonagh, Plunkett desecrated by the traitors, Collins etc. The wretched prison yard (Wing A)—the basement cells) sic., the rubbish accumulated in the dead space between wings A & B. The puddles after rain. The ring, railings, mud, puddles, rough clinker stones designed for punishment. The prisoners' shirts on the barbed wire—three or four prisoners with broken boots & ragged-ended trousers pacing around. The lags pushing a handcart escorted by a warden. The sense of closure & desolation, made more desolate by the sound of a guard's rifle shot & pigeons whirling madly around the ridge of the criminal building.

30 October 1922

They've killed our men, and now must kill our tunes—riflemen guards at night in the 'Circle'—'armed with rifles and mouth-organs.' (Frank G [*Gallagher?*])[9]—making the night hideous and the prisoners' sleep impossible with the old songs—'The West's Awake,' 'Kelly the Boy from Killann', 'The Felons of our Land'—utterly unconscious what those songs stand for—a row starts suddenly among them, loud words & a revolver shot. Then the hurried voice of an officer:—'Who fired that shot?'

Saturday 21 October 1922

Tuesday 31 October 1922, Hallow Eve

7.45 p.m. Just as the Fianna were getting ready to produce Pearse's play *Iosagan* and *Birthright* (2nd time) two F. S. policemen with revolvers came up to the stage and said, 'Take those blankets down, and be f—g quick about it!' Protests were made, but to no avail. The O/c Wing asked the Governor by note was the stopping of the play done with his sanction? He received back his note with the Governor's ukase—'no play'—written across it. All the prisoners moving about in the cold (how cold!) A1 landing with gloomy faces. There is not much heart among us, since the parcels were stopped. We are permitted to exist—to breathe—and no more.

Tuesday 31 October 1922 Hallow Eve Night

11 p.m. A quarter of an hour after 'lights out', a concert—organised by way of protest against the stopping of the plays—began. Each prisoner singer had a number beginning with 100. Sharply at 11 p.m. the number 100 was called out, &—began from his cell to sing 'Dark Rosaleen.' Great chorussing & applause at the end. He called 101 & D O' D—began 'The Battle-Hymn' (very well sung). Then 102 Joe Begley followed with the 'Fireship', Paddy M—'The Dawning of the Day', D—O'D 'Avenging and Bright', Led–, Q.M. Wing; 'The Rose of Tralee.' (A3); Mordaunt, 'The Workers Song'(Maryland) etc. etc. 'Wrap the Green Flag round Me.' Revolver shots began to ring out after Art O' Connor's[10] song. The guards in circle fired 5 times. Then after Paddy M –y's, two rifle shots were fired up the wing. I could hear the locks of the wing gates being opened & the guard crept up in canvas shoes into wing A1. '111!' 'If you don't stop your 111, I'll give you 303!' cried the guard. The singer stopped. Deathly stillness. Then a song & recitation could be heard far-off in the other wings & cheering. A 'jerry' was thrown down from A3 (against orders) followed by a bottle which smashed itself to pieces on A1 floor. The guard was changed & no further molestation took place. In fact, at the Soldiers' Song sung about 12-30 a.m. the guards below (I was told) stood to attention. All ended quietly with O/C's

shouted order: 'To sleep now lads. Parade at 7-50 in the morning & two minutes "stand to" in silence for second anniversary of Kevin Barry's hanging.'

1–2 November 1922

During the night (intensely cold wind blowing through cell window) I had a dream:—I dreamt that my right hand was cut (blown) suddenly off & that the Republicans under a leader with a Gaelic name like MacEachtaigh re-occupied the city of Galway & a cathedral. (I read in yesterday's paper (1 September 1922) that Clifden Barracks has been recaptured in ruins after 10 hours fighting.) I kept on thinking that the loss of my right hand from the wrist would be an honorable loss, received in the war for the Republic, & would be so looked on, especially by women;—but how would I write? I am a poet first, last and above all.

The ambush (between Loughlinstown & Cabinteely) Friday 14: July 1922.—Meeting M—(one of the ambushing party) in Mountjoy.

The blowing up of the D–[*Dargle*] Bridge.

The evacuation & burning of E–[*Enniskerry?*] Barracks

The night out with the road-blockers & tree fellers near the Scalp

3 November 1922—Friday

A tin of rice, ½ pint milk, piece of dry bread (without butter) for dinner today. A fine clear, cold, sunshiny day, inducing appetite. Everybody very cross & hungry. The primitive need of food.

Letter from Nancy:—

'Mr & Mrs N. of course—Gavin Duffy!![11] James Mc D—!! & the Gogartys! *Wasn't* I among the F. S.'s! Oh, poor Oliver[12]—he *did* seem glum. I believe he is fearfully bitter against the "Irregulars," & he'd hardly look at me. (Mrs. was quite friendly in her conventional way, & asked me to come in soon to see them.) I believe he was very upset at G–'s and M–'s deaths,[13] & then they can hear no news from Renvyle at all—think it may be burned– everyone has had to leave that part (all those parasitical big rich folk!!)[14] I put on a concerned & grieved look & talked platitudes. Oliver thawed a little towards the end—but, the poor man, he looked very droopy. (I thought afterwards his place would be passing on the latest witticism from the capital with Pontius Pilate, or flippantly discussing the real meaning of verity—while a shabby little procession was wending its way to Calvary. That's his sort of temperament.—"These d–d peasant disturbers! Leave me to my carved ivory statuettes & rare dishes."'

Not near and yet not far—some say at the Broadstone, others say at Marlboro' Barracks (British occupation) there is a machine-gun barking all day from early in the morning—tat -tat- tat—a few rolls & then two minutes silence. If one is inclined to forget that there is a war on, the gun is a constant reminder. 4 November 1922

Friday 1 a.m. 28 July 1922

When I was searched at the Governor's office on my entry into Mountjoy from Wellington Bks. the searcher turned out my purse, found one penny in it & said across to Paudeen,[15] who sat wise & humpbacked before his book taking down particulars: 'This man has no property.' 'No', I said across to D—the gunman who stood by: 'The poets are always penniless.'

My arrest by 'Chinny' M—on the fine summer evening of Friday 7: July: 1922. 'You're wanted over at the barracks. Come! push along that bicycle.' D—the grocer's assistant looked in at me where I sat in the iron-shuttered clink along with 3 ex-Tommies in for drunkenness & insubordination, & the ship's greaser who talked of Hong Kong & New York. In for looting. Beds on floor. Tolstoyan prisoners in 'War & Peace.'

12 July 1922

The drunken fishwoman & the guard at Bray Bridge Wednesday 12 midnight. Deep fishbaskets on either shawled arm. The cheers of the prisoners from the hotel windows. 'Up the Coombe!' The soldiers' jibes & laughing. A shot fired. ''Alt!' in the darkness.

The send-off from Bray. 14: July: 1922. The neutral (partly hostile) crowd on the outskirts. The gapers who came to look at us—the armoured car, the empty lorry, the lorry for the escorting troops. The faithful Cumann-na-mBan girls. The hands break-through the guard of riflemen. The hostile, glum looks of D—& the guard, the handshakes. The cheer as we moved away. 'Up the Republic!' The knots of poor women at their doors in Little Bray.

[*Copy of Letter*]
Cell 9: Wing A2,
Mountjoy Military Prison.
9 November 1922

A chara,

I beg personally to inform you that I have gone on hunger-and-thirst strike from 8.30 a.m. today (Thursday). My reason for taking this grave step is that for the past week I have not been getting the official prison rations as published in the press sometime ago. Last night after count, only one ration of milk was left in this cell for two prisoners. Tea and butter have been short all the week. As no parcels are allowed in from the outside, and as we are absolutely dependent on the food supplied by the prison authorities, the onus falls on you if my physical health breaks down. Never during the British occupation were Irish prisoners treated as they are today. Our status is no better than that of slaves. Many of the men in this Wing are in rags, & without boots. The pipes in my cell are, at the moment of writing, stone-cold. You might kindly inform my wife of my protest. Her address is either c/o 15 Marlboro Road, Dublin,[16] or c/o Mrs Howell, 5 Carlyle Square, Chelsea, London. S.W.

mise do chara
Joseph Campbell
The Military Governor
Mountjoy.

9 November 1922

4 p.m. Nothing to eat or drink since 8 p.m. last night. A bit weak & tottery. Dull headache. Taste in mouth. The first day of hunger-strike is largely an experience of nerves. Will settle down, I imagine. Several 'Job's comforters' in to see me. Washed 2 shirts & handkfs. Slept better than I thought (11 p.m.), but woke several times during night. Infernal din from guards in 'Circle' all night.

10 November 1922

Kept in bed until about 2 p.m. Prison M. O. (C–) in to see me. Told him I would cease hunger-strike if Governor gave me account of official ration & promise that each man would get his quantum. Very weak on legs. About 7-30 p.m. 3 Fianna Boys came in & told me they were thinking of going on hunger strike. Short rations & very hungry. Decided weakness about heart 8 p.m. Sent for prison M. O. 48 hours now without taking food.

[Nothing in the Diary suggests how the hunger-strike ended, but in October 1923 Campbell wrote that he had been on 48 hours' hunger-strike in Mountjoy.]

Wed. 15 November 1922

Word brought in today that Scully's cat was lying dead in the yard with four revolver bullets in it—Killed by F.S. guard. Alas, for so bad an end to Scully's cat 'Skipper (Nigger)'. How it used to lie on his bed in the cell—on its back with its legs spread out; how he used to scrounge milk—'There's a cat here!'—and fat meat for its dinner & breakfast. Cat fed first thing in the morning before Begley & he got up. How he'd shield it from the white-footed lady cat *'Cat na gcos mBán'* [the cat of the white feet] etc. Its nights out, in spite of all precautions. Alas! and alas!

16 November 1922 Cat not dead. Sleek, black, shiny, stretching on Joe Begley's bed! The whitefooted female 'mate' shot.

Saturday 18 November 1922

As Tom D–, Dom. Collins and I were washing A2 Landing this morning word came in—'Serious news! Four Republicans hanged in Kilmainham. The Government's last kick.' Everybody carrying the rumour. When I had finished & was cleaning myself up in my cell, Liam L –y came in & said the news was authentic. Four men of the names—Cassidy, Gaffney, Fisher, Tuohy.

Shot all right. A paper was coming in to O/C A MacD –d from B Wing. 'A Government that rests on hangings is pretty insecure.' Irishmen guilty of killing Irishmen—honourable men. Oh, God! as a race we are made up of utter light and utter darkness—saints & devils—children of extremes.

James Fisher (18) Echlin St. Dublin
Peter Cassidy (21) 7 Usher St.
Richard Tuohy (21) 1 O'Connors Bldgs (off James's St. Harbour)
John Gaffney (21) 3 Usher's St.[17]

Saturday 18 November 1922

News brought in by Sean Moynihan, who had it from D—O'D—, that Erskine Childers[18] and David Robinson[19] were to be executed on Monday. Everybody very serious—drawn, anxious faces. Can the wretched Provisional Govt. survive these executions? Tom Johnston[20] supposed to be for the executions, yet he could not understand why no notice was given of the executions of the 4 men in Kilmainham. Twelve hours elapsed after executions & before public informed. Kilmainham of unhappy memories for Ireland. Erskine Childers was a man they *hated—he seemed to attract* hate. F. S. Guard said that this would do for the P. G. [*Provisional Government*]—a good sign to see the rank & file dissatisfied.

Sunday 19 November 1922

A lovely, mild, misty, sunshining morning. Bells ringing for Mass. A feeling of sick horror, all the same, grips me because of these executions. Will Erskine Childers die tomorrow? Poor melancholy, strange-mannered Childers! The most hated man in Ireland—'a damned Englishman,' as Arthur Griffith called him. Today at 12 noon all the men in A wing were paraded & S–D–, orderly officer, read out—standing on the iron stairs—the names, addresses & history of the 4 executed men. Before the rosary was said I asked D– O'D– did he think they *would* execute Childers? He had his doubts if they would—spoke cryptically—something might happen. About 11-30 a.m. the sentry outside exercise yard fired two shots at prisoners—nobody hit. (*Independent* against executions—complains of censorship.)

In course of conversation one day with Robert Barton he told me that Griffith (while in London at the 'Peace' Conference) referred to me disparagingly.—'a crank & sorehead!' A compliment to have these things said about one by Griffith. It arose out of talk about the Sworn Inquiry into the Wicklow Co. Council business. John O'B—asked B—[*Barton*] 'Did he know Campbell?'

The word survives the deed it celebrates. Christ would be nothing but for the evangelists. The deeds of Finn, of Cuchulain, of Meave would be nothing but for the sagas of the poets. 19 November 1922

Thursday 23 November 1922

All the prisoners in A wing ordered out by Staters into yard about 2-30 p.m. A search of cells, it seemed. While outside in the cold foggy air we could hear beds, shelves, book-racks etc. being pitched into the compound. The doors for beds made a deafening racket as they hit the granite flags. It was dark night—6-30 p.m.—before we were readmitted. No tea—very hungry & cold. Personal search—hands held up—as we entered the compound. Found my cell topsy-turvy when I got in—books, boxes etc. littered over floor. A policy of annoyance, mean vindictiveness & degradation. Nothing like a shelf allowed.

Before darkfall, & as the beds & shelves were clattering down inside the closed prison door, I saw the Deputy Governor in close conversation with the R.C. Chaplain—tall-hatted with umbrella etc.—outside the ring railings next hospital. Over the prison building the new moon rose clear & white in a frosty sky. Old battered flag black in the hard moonlight on flag-pole. I suggested to D—O'D—that he should turn his money in his pocket & wish. 'All I have' said he in the frosty darkness 'is in my boots, and I can't get at it to turn!'

Thursday night: 9 o'clock or thereabouts 23 November 1922

A sudden burst—sharp crackle—of rifle-fire outside prison avenue—towards Mater Hospital it seemed. Crack!. Crack!—then silence—then crack!—silence—crack!, crack!, crack!, swelling into the intensity of a battle as the opposing forces began to engage. Boom!—a bomb thrown. The armoured car in yard began to purr & spurt—then it ran out with a harsh clanging of gears. Gurr-gurr-gurr!—the deep roll of a Lewis gun, followed by the sharp crackling splutter of a Thompson. Then a Vicars—belt, water-cooled as distinct from the drum, air-cooled—slow, deep, continuous. Then crack! crack!—the rifles going. Battle ends as suddenly as it began in the darkness. Crack! one shot after a long interval, then silence; & after a pause, the trams begin to hiss along the rails & overhead wires. 20 minutes. We sat listening intently to it all in No 9 cell.

Thursday night: 9-45 or thereabouts. 23 November 1922

Battle resumed, after an interval of lull, with increased intensity. Machine-gun duel lasting about half-an-hour, closer somewhat than before. Ending in Lancia car going out from yard—running feet—then silence—then a rifle shot & reply & silence.

Friday morning: 24 November 1922

Rumours of a general 'hit-up' in Dublin. All F. S. posts attacked according to stories going the rounds of A wing. S. Moynihan (out in baths for sulphur-bath) saw part of Vicars gun damaged; also Lancia car riddled & pitted with bullet marks. F.S. soldier wounded hand.

24 November 1922 Friday

About 4-30. p.m.—just as we came in from exercise yard for tea—news going the rounds that Erskine Childers & 8 others were executed Thursday morning. Was this reason for 'hit-up' on Thursday night?

Personally, I felt sick with feeling of horror all evening. A black Christmas for us & for Ireland. Oh God! how will it all end? What do the people outside really think? Where is Ireland's reputation for humanity & decency? What of the Church? Is the public conscience paralysed & inert that no stay can be set to it at all? These men's bodies lie cold in the grave—but their spirit—what of it? Can the F. S. 'Government' survive its initial rottenness?

Saturday 25 November 1922

Clear sunshiny day after a night's frost. The sun on our side of A wing shining clear through bars of cell window & duplicating them as shadows on wall opposite. As a prisoner remarked, 'I don't like to see the sun in a prison cell. It has a cold, inhuman look—*not* like home.' *[Added apparently later:]* We had no reason to rejoice at this time owing to the executions & our hard lot in prison without privileges of any kind—only bare food & snatches of sleep.

25 November 1922 *Food & Sleep*—necessities of life. We have a minimum of both.—At night, owing to the racket of the guards in 'Circle', one only gets sleep in snatches; & the cells are liable to be entered at any hour. Not a nice sensation to wake up from mattress on floor & in the uncertain gloom to see a great-coated policeman with drawn revolver standing over one!

Sat. 25 November 1922

While standing at A wing Gate today, waiting for food to come through, I saw one of the lags cut off a piece of butter—about 1lb or so—from piece weighed out for one of the landings, put it on piece of newspaper, wrap it up quickly & tuck it into the wooden box on which scales stood. For himself, or warder? So we are prisoners defrauded of our food.

26 November 1922

It is obvious now that Erskine Childers was executed at the order of the English Cabinet. The four unknown young men were done to death (as the Prov 'Govt.' Ministers said in their speeches) to prepare the public—to take the edge off the shock, as it were. England has always been venomous against what she calls 'renegades' (Casement is an example). Extraordinary turn of fortune—the man who ran the guns at Howth in Aug. 1914 & made 1916 & what followed possible, should die by the guns of Irish 'rebels'. (Casement's exposure of Capitalism: Childers' exposure of British inner political methods) Like the judges in the Salem witchcraft trials they have won 'an immortality of infamy'.[21]

'The same crimes, against the same victims, by the same methods, for the same motives, with invocations of the same shibboleths, age, after age. Change the labels; that is all. New scenery and costumes; the same old stage & tragedy.' Lucien Price (Salem Witches)

N. Y. *Nation* 4 October 1922

The Night-Light—made from the fat of the day's dinner—enabled me to read 'Meredith's Letters', 'The Vision of Dante' (Cary) etc. etc. 'Twentieth Century Lyrics'—shadows on wall, obscurity, mystery.

Shorter lyrics of the 20th Century.[22] I was considered worthy to be of the number of the poets—but the F. S. threw me into prison. Not the first poet to languish in a prison, by any means.

The Prison Bibles—propping beds, used for lavatory paper etc. My request to Joe Begley for an untorn copy from his assortment. 'I'll swop an unmutilated copy for two others to go under my bed.' Old Mick Fleming's knowledge of the Scriptures got while doing 6 months in Tralee Prison during the Plan of Campaign.[23]

1 December 1922

Through the open bars of the lavatory window A2 I saw this morning a most wonderful cloud—white, iridescent, goldeny in the clear sunlight. How slowly it sailed by—from what free celestial country? Beginning of fatal month for Ireland—month in which the 'articles of agreement' (?) were signed.[24]

Sat. 2 December 1922

Awoke this morning (7.50 a.m.) with the sound of Berkely Rd or St. Peter's bell in my ears for 8 Mass. The overtones & undertones & their effect on my senses. The 'body' of the bell was the ore of (apparent) reality; the overtones (continuous hum of sound like the drones in bagpipes) were the continually elusive, the eternal. Ireland's fate, somehow, seemed mixed up in the sounds.

'F–k, fight & drink porter!'

3 December 1922 Sunday 12 midnight

About 20 past twelve midnight, as I was dozing over to sleep, I was wakened up suddenly with the confused trampling of many men in the Compound below. Not a rhythmical tramp, but the heavy tread of military-booted feet. I shouted over to M. that there was something 'up'. Then I heard the order passed along A1 cells:– 'Now lads, up. Dress yourselves & put on your boots'. Then there was a further order to get up to A2 Landing. M—got up, but I stayed in bed until I knew further. I thought it might be an order to get up & shift quarters to the Curragh or elsewhere. *Very cold* night. They had discovered the tunnel! One of the searchers was in singlet & drawers. The noise & clatter went on until 2-20 a.m. when the O/C fell the A1 men in below & they got back to their beds. Guards put on two cells. General 'wind-up'! Did not sleep for a long time & that only in dozes.

27 July 1922

The drive through Dublin on the night of our removal from Wellington to Mountjoy. The 2 lorries & escort. The peeps from under the canvas-covered lorries [*interlined: tenders*] at the deserted streets. An odd D.M.P.[25] man. The ruins of the G. P. O. and the hotel area. Shattered old city—the Customs Ho., Four Courts etc.

'I think of Fighting Men' (go over the fighting men of history—and what better, who more heroic against fearful odds than the Men of the Columns?) The Fianna—the 'gods & fighting men'—are far-off & it is safe to write about them—but I will celebrate the heroism of my contemporaries.

'That old one would breed from a lick of your trousers, as they say.' (T. Byrne)

6 December 1922 Wednesday

Fatal anniversary of the signing of the Articles of 'Agreement.'[26] What rivers of blood between Irishmen! What a legacy of bitterness & war! What example of treachery for our children! 'You have split the Irish people from top to bottom—and Lloyd George[27] knew it'. (letter to Arthur Griffith). Founded on dishonour, built with corruption—how long will the building stand?

6 December 1922

Clear, bitter-frosty evening. Marching round the Ring in the incipient blue winter dusk (with 2 other prisoners) I saw Scully's cat outside the railings next the Guard Room—balked by a tangle of rusty barbed wire—from getting at a flock of sparrows which had alighted to pick up some bread scattered by the sentry. Ears pricked, tail twitching restlessly—a picture of baffled hope. It relied on the rapidity of its spring to dart in on them, but was foiled by the wire—delicate pads of feet would be torn etc.

7 December 1922

The architects of the 'Free' State—Collins & Griffith—by a miraculous interposition of providence have gone. So surely as I write this will the Free State go itself. Dishonour is a bad foundation to build on.

7 December 1922

If I ever felt unconvinced that Mountjoy was Hell, I am convinced today. Such a pandemonium of metallic sound in the Circle! Old pipes, bars, scrap of all kinds from one of the Wings is being removed. Oh! God keep me sane in mind through it all—the Powers of Darkness gird me round about.

Thursday 7 December 1922

As I was washing mugs at A2 Lavatory before going to bed (10 p.m.) was told that Sean Hales & Padraic O Maille[28] had been fired at as they were getting on a hack car outside Exchange Hotel. First killed, second wounded.

'How do you mean?' 'H-h-ow? Not so much of my dear F-frank. H-h-hump off out of my cell!' Blue-black shiny hair. Pugnacious face. Queer dry ironic humour. Chess. Cards. Savonarola.

Friday 8 December 1922 (Feast of Immaculate Conception)

I have ceased to believe in the God of orthodox religion. Rory O'Connor, Liam Mellowes, Joe McKelvey & Dick Barrett[29] were taken out from C. Wing & shot about 9-20 o clock this morning. I heard the volley which killed them. It was so loud at first that I thought it must be an explosion somewhere. But it had not the depth of sound of bomb or mine—just rifle-shots in unison. About 12 revolver shots were heard following. The first I heard of the executions was when M. & T. B. came into my cell from Mass (Holyday of Obligation). 'Did I hear the news?' they said, T. B.'s eyes startled, & his face an ashen-white colour. 'God have mercy on them—they were brave men,' I said. It seems they had been informed about 2 a.m. that they were to be removed that morning. Told to pack up their things. The young priest at Mass, visibly moved, simply announced: 'Mass will be offered for 4 of your brave comrades (giving names) who went to meet their Maker about ten minutes ago.' (Mass had been considerably delayed. A priest was seen running back with a Prayer Book, as if he had been called hurriedly to officiate. The prison M. O., Loftus, at Mass looking white & strained. Received Communion. Probably he had certified the men as dead.)

Fri. 8 December 1922

'The execution took place this morning at Mtjoy Jail of the following persons taken in arms against the Irish Govt. (names) as a reprisal for the assassination on his way to Dáil Eireann on the 7th Dec. of Brig. Sean Hales T.D. & as a solemn warning to those associated with them who are engaged in a conspiracy of assassination against the representatives of the Irish people.' Official announcement from Free State G. H. Q.

3 clergymen were in attendance. The prisoners were marched together to the scene (wall back of red shed near Hospital). They were blindfolded. Bodies buried soon afterwards inside prison grounds. 3 coffins brought in at midnight; 3 graves dug. (The digging of the graves in the darkness. The men for whom they were intended, still alive.)

Friday 8 December 1922

Out of their sleep, at two—inhuman hour—
Into the gaslit gloom, with padded feet,
They dragged them to be murdered.

(The 4 men were informed by their Guards who awakened them that they were to be shifted: a long journey they went on! Told to pack up. Guards helped them to pack. Removed to Female Wing before execution)

Friday 8 December 1922

I went out this afternoon (had headache & aching spirits from morning's ghastly happenings) into the Ring for some air & exercise. Gloomy December dusk. Sky misted, with pinkish glow over chimney-tops, & over the long Female Wing a pile of yellowish, dusky cumulus cloud. Ground very wet—great puddles of muddy water reflecting yellowish clouded light from sky. There had been a lot of rain during the morning ('to wash away the bloodshed,' some prisoner said, 'like the rain after the executions in Easter Week'). Prisoners going round in aimless depressed groups, talking over the morning's work in low voices. General opinion that the Republic will not be beaten by such methods—blame of the Church etc. Anarchy will be the fruit of the 'articles of Agreement.' The day of the prisoner of Hades will surely dawn.

Friday 8 December 1922

As I came in darkness had fallen. Guards jangling their keys in the gloom. No lights (or few—3 or 4—in compound.) Prisoners moving about like figures in a Cyclops' forge (Vulcan's stithy)[30]—with flaring pieces of paper to light the gas in their cells. (Or like workers in a bottle factory). The sight gave me a curious aesthetic 'lift'—suggested Wagner's music, somehow. Confused babel of voices—prisoners at doors waiting for tea—tin mugs being rattled together. Clarke's voice bawling (as if being strangled!) in A1. Oh, God save Ireland from further horrors! We have supped full enough.

Saturday morning 9 December 1922

Slept badly from 4 a.m. Heard the *evil* noises of early morning—jangling of keys, banging of the gate, jarring of gate lock, the uncanny heavy rubber-padded tramp of the guards up & down the Compound, the racket of milk cans about 7 a.m., the whirring racket of the basement chain, slamming of wooden trays by the 'lags' starting their day's work—at 6 a.m. a chapel bell tolling for Mass (ironic commentary on it all). No sparrows this morning at the cell window. All foggy gloom—psychic as well as physical.

Ireland is a hot desert of sand into which blood is poured. Seven centuries of pouring. It still thirsts for more—& the more disappears. When will it have drunk its fill of blood? When will the bloody manuring bear fruit?

(Nearly 6 months after!!—28th June—10th December 1922)

'A week has passed since the first shots were exchanged in this most tragic & wanton conflict, which is now happily nearing a conclusion.'

Kevin O'Sheil[31] in *The Free State* 8 July 1922

'No compensation can repay the Nation for the loss of her records which were totally destroyed in the flames of the Four Courts—records dating from the twelfth century . . . it will be discovered some day that European culture has suffered no greater blow since the burning of Louvain University than the destruction of those priceless documents.'

do. do. 8 July 1922

(Ye Gods! documents validating spoliation & conquest of the actual soil of Ireland by foreigners & bodachs, who since their occupation have done their worst to bleed the nation white) What have these people contributed to culture?

'Tá an troid thart anois' [The battle is over now.]

Pádraic Ó Conaire[32] in *The Free State*,

July 8 1922

(Is it, Padraic?

10 December 1922)

Thursday 14 December 1922

Word just brought in (5 p.m.) that an undertaker's van had brought a coffin into the Hospital about 5 minutes before. Who is it for? Who is to go next? The French Revolution pales before this.

Thursday 14 December 1922

This morning about 6 o'clock I heard the lowing of cattle & the shouts of drovers going towards the Dublin Cattle Market (ditto Thursday before Christmas).

I had a strange dream the other night. Shelley came to me & told me not to be fearful. I saw him like a sort of Angel. He said that I was of the company of the poets & not to fear anything. 'If I had not been drowned,' he said 'I would have died on the scaffold. Castlereagh would have killed me.'[33] It all seemed so real & corporeal, somehow.

Sunday 17 December 1922

If one is going to do anything that matters, one must do it alone. One cannot go into rebellion with one's wife; or face a firing-squad with one's dearest friend. Christ on his 40 days fast—alone when the Devil came to him; [Garden of Gethsemane] alone on Golgotha; Dante in exile; Pearse; Casement.('Good Deeds' in *Everyman*.)

Thursday night 7 p.m. 14 December 1922

Word brought in that letters for prisoners had been admitted to the Wing. About 8 p.m. the landing Adjutant came along & handed me in the cell seven letters—6 from Nancy, 1 from Padraic Colum.[34] 'For this relief much thanks.'

Friday 15 December 1922

Parcels readmitted after stoppage on 10th Oct. There is a general feeling of relief in A wing. We have sighted land again after a dangerous & tempestuous voyage. We have arrived at the edge of the forest—can see the light—after our long journey, torn by boughs & lost in twilight. The prisoners congregate in hilarious groups. Every other man is smoking a cigarette—hundreds of red tips in the gloom of the compound. Jimmy Donnelly's a smoking Vesuvius of tobacco fumes. Tables near gates at which the Adjutants sit checking off names as battered (& pilfered) parcels are handed out. Much bawling of missing prisoners' names. Men who have had fallings-out shake hands & talk again. Bells ring for tea orderlies. A Christmas feeling in the air.

Saturday 16 December 1922

Not yet out of the wood. B wing is on hunger-strike for 4 days owing to removal of its O/C to basement. Trouble with signers of forms for release. The hunger-strikers held a concert tonight. Great cheering. Revolver-shots fired over their heads—seven or eight of them at intervals—by guards. Chivvied into cells rather unceremoniously in A wing. Lights turned off suddenly 10.30 p.m. General windiness. 'Bad crowd on.'

Monday 18 December 1922

Cold wintry morning, with high wind, after all night's rain. Ring in great muddy puddles & slippery mud. I saw 4 lags in charge of a warder dragging out a heavy wooden bogey with 3 wooden iron-shod wheels—wheels not even round, creaking on wobbly axles—the lags with 2 crosscut saws. What a picture of degradation & futility! Logs for the Christmas fire?! God help erring & blind humanity.

Tuesday 19 December 1922

(The flag over the jail very black against the white glow of the December sun; stiff & flat in a sharp breeze from the north.)

The Sunspot
Black against the bright December sun,
The flag that was the Tricolor stood stiff
Stiff in an evil wind, stubborn with shame;

Black with a blackness more than of rain-mixed soot, winter blackness, psychic blackness; its springtime colours of green & white & orange—the colours of Pearse & MacDonagh—gone. What earthquake, what ill to Ireland does the sunspot portent?

25 December 1922 *Christmas Day in Jail*

The feast in Joe Begleys' cell. 4 p.m. 13 present—and the black cat Nigger. The gaslight on the tables set end on end—fragments of cold chicken—cake—brilliant oranges. Joe's head & shoulders in shadow—pince-nez glancing occasionally—the talk & merriment—Scully in blue overalls helping—his cheery, stubborn face—toothless etc.

Rumour that 'Specials'[35] had occupied the 3 F. S. Ulster Counties, Donegal, Cavan, Monaghan. Old Moore for 1923 prophesies that 600 prisoners are to be slaughtered in Irish jails. 'Jail used to be called a safe place, but it isn't so now.'—G. B.

8 January 1923

Today a young fellow from Tipp. town came to see me with two doggerel verses & asked me would I complete the 8th line for him—'stuck in it,' he said. 'Poetry always breaks out, like scabies, in jail' as Joe Begley said. The 'poet's' ingenuousness & respect for a real bard.

30–31 December 1922

Sunday morning 2 a.m. awakened out of my sleep by what I thought was the noise of the parade for Mass. Later a F. S. soldier came in with O/C wing, scanned a paper over, but neither my name nor my cellmates was on it. Over 80 prisoners from A wing (300 in whole prison) to be removed—to a Camp? Hare Park, Newbridge? Great excitement & packing in gaslit December gloom. Songs from Paddy Morrissey & the O/C ('Felons of our Land' etc.) Prisoners paraded with boxes, parcels, kits etc. How often has this scene been enacted in Ireland! ('Bodyke eviction', as Rinn the school master said to me). Prisoners file out slowly in twos for search & hand-cuffing. Outside in Main Yard, whirring & sputtering of motors—great chaos—repeated at a distance outside. Chapel bells ringing for Mass. Evacuation apparently delayed, as they would not move prisoners in broad daylight, as they did.

1 January 1923

New Year's Eve

Lying awake on mattress in darkness, heard (1st) church bells clanging & chiming in New Year. Then (2nd) horns & sirens of shipping at North Wall. Then (3rd) banging of mugs, hammering of bars etc.—with shouting & singing in A3 &, at a distance, in other wings. Then (4th) after the bulk of the commotion had died down, rapid rifle fire in Berkley Rd. direction—sputter, sputter—& reply. The New Year had dawned for Ireland!

3 January 1923 D Wing

Just heard that 'Giller', 'Monty', Johnny Pigeon & Mordaunt (Bolshy) had been put into cells in B. Basement, & bashed about by guards, because it was discovered that they had not gone to Newbridge (as they ought to have) on Sunday 30–31 Dec., but had let others go in their names.

A feeling of emptiness & 'left-behindness' in A Wing. At 2-30 Simon Donnelly[36] called out:– 'Everybody pack up & be ready by 2-30 p.m.' Later the order came: 'Bedding, utensils etc to be packed, too.' Everybody busy with their bundles. At 2-30 p.m. the compound was littered with packs of blankets etc. Prisoners hung around in talking & excited groups, with overcoats, hats and mufflers on. The Deputy Governor (pale & truculent) came in with other officers about 3 p.m. All prisoners whose names began with A, B & C were paraded at end of landing;

then marched up to gates. I was laden down with my mattress & blankets, plate, mugs, dish & 2 kits of personal effects, books etc. Various rumours on the round that we were not going to the Curragh, but only to be transferred to C. Wing. I gave my name to the Deputy Governor, but it was not on his list. 'Stand aside,' he said. 'Am I for execution?' I said, laughing, to Seán Burke who was also 'reserved.' Eventually I was told to go to D Wing, whither I lugged my belongings in 2 journeys escorted by a pistolled guard. D. prisoners in crowds behind their gates. As I came through & the gates were banged after me, I said 'Another wild beast for the menagerie!' General laughter. Put into 11 cell on D1—which I didn't like, as it was dark, dirty, & smelly. Went up to D2, foraged & found a clean cell in No 4—in which I am ensconced for the time being, praises be! No cell-mate so far. The A wing prisoners were scattered over B, C & D wings promiscuously. Most of the men belonging to our Irish class are, luckily, in D Wing.

2 January 1923

D Wing, (describe its dirt, pool of water with bread & garbage, papers etc. at door end, leading out to Hang House.) The condemned cells—fire-place, archway, chairs, distempered unaesthetic green & red walls, water over floors from lavatories; heavy smell. The Hang House outside. Stone steps with iron railing out to exercise yard. Square, with high wall & wall of Wing—with rows of windows, small & barred—concrete paths for exercise, 3 of them concentrically. Wire, wire everywhere: Workshops & rifled sentry sitting between it & wire cage. Main gateway towering over wall (grass-grown, with wire, on top). Chimney towers. Dirty flag—all colour out of it with rain & soot. Sentry with gun on archway top. Walled-in feeling. Pools of muddy water in yard—a dust-bath in summer—slime oozing in yellow iridescent ooze from rusty-padlocked doorway steps.

The Hang House—D Wing

Glimpse thro' hole cut in door at head of stone steps. Crack in brick arch over door. The glass-lighted roof, beam, whitewashed brick walls—the trapdoors hanging down into fatal pit. Souvenirs hacked off the floor by Republican prisoners of C. Wing. (Four Courts men.) Levers broken. Here Kevin Barry, Moran, Whelan etc. were hanged.[37] Aura of sin & heroism. The condemned cells in D wing, spyholes in wall (not in doors). Window from yard looking into hang-pit bricked up. Door. [Steps from floor of hang-house down to pit] [The iniquity of it—hidden away from sight—the Church—accumulated dirt and garbage at bottom].

2 January 1923

The Gaelic Class in Condemned Cell. Gaslight. Walls of green & red. Ashy fireplace—fire unlit. Foul smell. Water over floor from D2 latrine. Wall damp from water of D3 latrine above. The horrible aura of the room. Broke panes of windows with legs of stool. The aura of Hynes. Describe the fine pale-faced upstanding man, Carleton-like[38] brow, mobile shaven mouth, deep voice, breeches & black leggings. The speech—wild, free-vowelled, ancient—of Glenbeigh & Dingle. Tang of salt & tang of heather & broken ground & cattle grazing by the sea under the mountains. O'Tuama from Ballyvourney. The other types. One aura struggling against the other—the Gaelic won.

Wed. 10 January 1923

About 10-30 300 prisoners were brought in from Athlone, Custume Barracks, mostly lads from Roscommon, Sligo, & Mayo. Splendid young men—some in battered uniform, leggings, boots, hats & trench coats covered with mud. Some wearing beards. All tired & sleepy. Knocked out of bed at Custume Barracks at 11 p.m. (just after they had got in at 10.30 p.m. lights out) kept standing out in rain all night until 4 a.m. when they were removed to train at Athlone. Got off 5 a.m. Marched from Broadstone to Mountjoy (no transport). Kept waiting 2 hours outside jail gate—searched in sixes. Lined up in D. Wing, they looked a splendid rough lot of Western men. Out all through the winter in the Columns—no returning home once they had gone out. The salt of Ireland. (How like all prisoners of war really look—fed up, unfed, unshaven, dirty, sleepy). Dr. Fearon T.D. & Professor McDevitt among them. Great hub-bub in D Wing getting them into cells, bedding, plates, mugs—we are 3 in a cell now, accommodation 10 × 7 only for 1 man. 388 prisoners in D wing. Congested district.

11 January 1923

After a disturbed night—3 in No 4 cell D2, 2 Sligo boys, one a motor-driver, & myself, the 2 men with dirty old mattresses & 2 *pieces* of blanket to cover them—a lovely sunny January morning. The boy from Lissadell seemed refined & beauty-loving—a quiet boy, not heavy-breathed like his mate: 'There'll be a bitter score to pay for all this,' he said as he brushed his jacket. Then, sadly: 'Oh, isn't it a pity to have us locked up!' All the freedom of the fields & the sea-washed strand of Lissadell & the far-off blue mountains was in that remark. 'If we only had a clean bed, itself'.

13 January 1923

Lines of Western & other prisoners in D wing gloom for count. As the Deputy Gov. passed along somebody started to whistle 'Bonny Kate.' Deputy put off count. Very irritable. Started to harangue D. 2 men in Cork accent. 'We'd no trouble here until men from Galway—that famous town that beat the Black & Tans. At your bloody peril no whistling.' Roars of laughter. 'In plain English, no *fucking* whistling.' Further screams of laughter.

Friday. 19 January 1923

Report that 4 men caught in an ambush last night outside Prison Gate were brought into B. basement & the usual maltreatment meted out to them. News per Liam O'D—of Jim Larkin's release from Sing Sing & prospective return to Ireland.[39] What will the official Labour crowd do? Long talk with S—, a Sligo prisoner about the situation in the West. Graphic firsthand description of the Dooney Rock ambush (Co Sligo) & capture & renaming of 'The Wild Rose of Loch Gill.' *Freeman*[40] version of 22 September 1922, he says, so much fiction. F. S. propaganda so much lying. The Column of 21 men—8 felling trees in

Markree Wood, rest cached in rocks over road, distant sound of Lewis gun fire—column on qui vive. Armoured car (F.S.) dashes up. Pulls up to engage tree-fellers—4 men jump out of rear of car—fusillade on them from rocks above. Retreat into car. (Fight going on with F.S. troops in lorries higher up road). Car hoists white flag of surrenders. Handed over to leader of column. In the meantime the other lorries have lost 36 men killed, wounded & surrendered. General congratulations. Priests sent for to attend the dying. (Priests hostile to Republicans). Owing to narrowness of road found difficulty in turning armoured car. At last success—triumphal return of column with car to Sligo—cheers from townspeople.[41]

Saturday 20 January 1923

The old dirty flag (potato-sack!) which has eclipsed the sun has been removed for some days & has not been replaced by a new tricolor. Has the British Colonial Office ordered the tricolor not to be flown any more? Looks like it. Griffith said: 'We have brought back the flag.' 'Which flag?'

20 January 1923

'They'll know us outside by the wheels & circles we'll take on the footpath. There'll be no walking in a straight line for us. We'll be striking the kerb every few minutes.'

Monday 22 January 1923

Rumoured that the 4 men caught on Thursday night (18th Jan)—see page 198—were caught in a tunnel being dug from Glengariffe Parade towards C. Wing—Medical Students (*All* 'Medicals' seem to be Republican). Very near success, but alas! *not* successful. 'Four yards only to go' said one of the sentries in exercise yard to a prisoner. 'Bogies and all working in it—a great tunnel.' Started, it seems, two months ago. 'They'll be plugged, poor devils!' Report that they were moved—6, not 4—out of A wing to Basement B. cells. Are they to be executed?

Monday 28 January 1923

Dr Frank Murray visited me in bed in No 4 cell D2 & said that I had tonsillitis. Slight temperature. Feeling rather mizzed. Prison M. O. O'Connor later. Moved to hospital just before 'count'—5 p.m. Went over with 2 other prisoners from B. & C. Wing. Melancholy standing about in circle, surrounded by revolvered police—gas-lit gloom of January evening. One poor prisoner from C. Wing (Robert Duggan) very pale & emaciated with a barking cough—lung gone. Passed along high walls past other wings to Hospital in darkness, guided by policeman—who, decently enough, carried my kit-bag for me. (Touch of human nature). Entered hospital by door opposite A 'Ring'—queer, 'iodiney' hospital smell. Went up to ward where we were received by the little Bon Secour, Sister Angela[42]. Got into bed next to Duggan. Later another young prisoner brought in (carried) by medical orderlies—very sick, with same complaint as myself. Spent uncomfortable, sleepless night—don't like to be sick myself or to have sick people near me. Throat still sore in morning, but better on the whole. Amusing chatter from beds before 'lights out'. Left hospital cured on Sunday night about 8 p.m.—halted by sentry in darkness. 'Advance one—to be recognised'.

Sunday morning 4 February 1923

Better of my attack of tonsillitis. Rose up & dressed & went off with four other convalescent prisoners (Mulkerns, the Dublin youth captured in the Glengarriffe Parade Tunnel) & went to Mass 7.30 a.m. Fine sunny spring morning. Passed the new graves of Rory O'Connor, Liam Mellows, Joe McKelvey & Dick Barrett—an oblong piece of ground in angle formed by two outbuildings, one the F.S. guardroom. Iron fencing posts & wire framed it in. New earth flattened over it—25 ft × 8 ft or so it looked. Sides of earth battered up with spades flush with fencing. Sentries with fixed bayonets. Went through entrance & into circle escorted by policeman. Paudeen & a big number of F. S. police ('bad buggers'—red faced, revolvered, be-legginged) in circle. Paudeen pale faced, humped, truculent, glowering—out with himself, as usual (evil conscience). Stood for a long time in circle waiting on prisoners from various wings to pass through to Mass. (D & C passing out, A & B passing in.) Nodded to by prisoners from the landing above. Saw Monty Lee coming out of A wing (punishment wing)—very pale & thin after his experience in B. Basement. Usual hugger-mugger ceremony of Mass. Priest hostile & remote from realities in his sermon. Got no religious or aesthetic thrill. Cold, breakfastless, early morning look on prisoners—shaven heads, zinc ointment on chins etc. As I came out, old basement chain began to rattle—'Porridge up!' Paudeen shouting at prisoners lingering about talking—only chance of friends to meet from other wings to which they were sent from A wing after 5 months of it. Paudeen suddenly ran out with revolver & shouted at young Joe Woods: Now then, Woods—get along! (Cork accent). When I got back young Sister Angela was in the hospital—came in every morning about 10 a.m. Soft nun's hands, young spectacled face, teeth, eyes, Bon Secours frill etc. Took 'exercise' on grass square—P.A. & sentry with rifle. Prisoners in B Wing exercise ring marching around. No one out in A. Ring—prisoners locked in their cells. Went in & read.

Tuesday 6 February 1923 Cell 14 D2

About 1 a.m. was awakened out of sleep by storm, blowing in gusts through open cell window (No. 14 D 2). All the night previous the gas was blown out repeatedly. Squalls of rain. Then whirring of lorries & cheers—repeated again & again—from Cumann na mBan girls apparently being shifted from their quarters in the Hospital. 'The Soldiers' Song' & other national songs sung—could hear the cheers & songs between the gusts of wind. As the lorries drove through the main gate there was a great hip-hip-hurrahing—poor brave girls in the rain, wind & darkness. What an impression! & what times! Upward of 70 girls were in the Hospital. Shrill, soprano cheers—like boys' cheering.

Wed 13 February 1923

Ash Wednesday

(Shrove Tuesday passed without me knowing it was Shrovetide! No pancakes.) Young Joe Woods brought me up a little dust of 'blessed ashes' in a piece of newspaper while I lay in bed awaiting breakfast. 'The priest sent them up to the men that are in bed. Wash your face & put some on your forehead!' Poor innocent Joe! To me these ashes are not more holy than any other ashes. *All* matter is 'blessed' as it is the Divine Spirit manifest. Are there not enough 'blessed ashes' in Ireland already as it is? I will keep the 'blessed ashes' all the same, as I am not irreverent.

Sat 16 February 1923

Was called out today to office re a letter from Nancy complaining of non-delivery to me of a parcel handed in at gate 25 January 1923. Group of prisoners at gate, as I went out, 'Are you for the ball-alley?' meaning execution. As I went through the barred gate into corridor, escorted by revolvered policeman, I was confronted by four young men in 'civvies'—Homburg hats, blue nap & fawn overcoats—well dressed—*with the most sinister faces*. What were they? & what did they there? *These sinister faces persist through history*—one can imagine them at all times of trouble & persecution—the days of Joan of Arc, of the Borgias, the Inquisition, the stakes of the Reformation, '98 etc. etc.

[Campbell was transferred to the Curragh (No. 2 Internment Camp Tintown) on 20 February 1923.]

Wed. 7 March 1923

Bitter, raw March day. P.J. Ryan *dixit* in wash-house:—'March has on his fighting gear this morning, Joseph!' 'Ay, P.J.—and he's using it.' Bitter wind sweeping—with rain-squalls—across open Curragh plain. Tin huts and muddy roads of camp very desolate. About 11.30 Seán Ó Caomhánaigh[43] (of Dunquin, Co Kerry) accosted me in Hut 12. Long talk about Starkey[44], the Hermit Parker, Padraic Colum, Padraic O Conaire & *literati* generally. Prize-fighter's face—mobile, humorous, Bohemian—one gold-crowned tooth, sign of American experience. Had seen 'Shorter Lyrics of 20th Century' (with my name in it, in Hut

1, with Eamonn Enright).—Spy-hunt in camp in afternoon. Some bricks thrown at gate. Coal-orderlies deprived of coal for stove 4 (Hut 12) in consequence. No fire, alas! and it bitterly cold. Scrounged coal from other stoves, broke up boxes etc. for fuel. Will we get our usual evening comfort of porridge & mug of tea? Great smashing of boxes after rosary—Seán Ó Tuama (Camp Commdt.) leading the van.

Sun. 9 March 1923 ANTHRAX

Informed by Hut Leader (Garraghan) this evening that the sheeting boards was not to be removed from Roof-Pillars as the horses stalled in Hut before during British Occupation of Curragh had suffered from *ANTHRAX*!!!—& the prisoners were liable to get the disease. Glanders etc. microbes in woodwork of stables.

Sat. 10 March 1923

A day of general upset. Locked in Hut 12 until about 3-30 p.m. No breakfast or dinner. The Camp Commdt. (Seán Ó Tuama) called out by F.S. orderly at 10 a.m. & not seen since. We sat round fireless stoves, getting more restless as the day wore on. Bitter, raw, cold March day—dry luckily, but sky grey & overcast. Ate about a pound of raw flake meal to stave-off hunger—'feed of oats'. About 2-30 p.m. scantlings out of roof & from posts supporting roof began to be removed & broken up. A free-fight had occurred earlier between P.J. Ryan & a western prisoner over a board for a shelf which P.J. claimed as his property. I remarked that the men were like cattle in a shed that had not been foddered or watered or let out. Restless, aimless wandering to & fro, or sullen standing-about, with hands in pockets. Then the men began to puck & shoulder each other & free fights became a general occurrence. Cries of 'Wind up! Wind up!' as someone got out his rag. (Humans in a crisis behave remarkably like animals. Grab food. Lose their altruism etc.) Men began poking their heads thro' windows & shouting to men in like plight in Huts 11 & 13. I felt as if we were in an ark, & had got ashore on rocks. At 3-30 we were released—marched out with mugs, plates, knife, fork & spoon over to F.S. Headquarters

Hut (where we had been examined on coming into the camp on the 20: Feb) Herded in a chaotic crowd (no semblance of military formation) a space back from a table at which sat a man in 'civvies' (a Civil Servant I heard afterwards) the Deputy-Governor in uniform, chocolate braids & gold band on sleeve & various P.A. men & orderlies in 'civvies'. As the names were called out three or four—including Wilmot & P.J. Ryan—answered them & stood to one side. Then silence. Men sullen & discontented. Shuffling feet, noise, calls of 'We want our breakfast!' A prisoner in a queue lined up outside from another hut shoved his head through window opposite officers' table & bawled: 'Give us our breakfast!' The Governor, ratty, replied: 'I'll give you your *breakfast*'. None of the officers displayed guns—but usual armed guard outside barbed wire. More shuffling & whispered consultation: we agreed not to answer our names until we had an opportunity of consulting with our Commdt. Seán Ó Tuama sent for. Came in looking worried & pale. Little speech: 'God knows you've suffered enough, without food or fire. Answer your names & numbers as they are called out.' Business began. Men filed led past as names were read out. General confusion as to numbers. My name called. '970!' I joined the crowd outside walking to & fro inside barbed wire compound. Bitterly cold. After endless waiting lined up according to our Huts & marched to Dining Hall No. 6. Fell on—literally fell on—dinner of roast beef & potatoes. Tea given us afterwards. Everybody in uproarious good-humour—complete change from morning. Marched back to Hut 12. Coal brought over by orderlies—buckshee buckets, too. (The camp organisation completely out of gear—& everybody from Governor to P.A. man in charge of coal at sixes & sevens & did as he liked). 'All's well that ends well!' Sat round stove at end of Hut 12 talking over day's doings. To bed 11 p.m. or thereabouts.

Sat 10 March 1923

12 midnight

Just as I was dozing off, wakened out of my sleep by electric light being suddenly switched on. A search party, headed by the Governor, entered. 'Stableman' had an iron bar. Went around all the beds. Lifted boots & peered into them. Glanced under beds. The long Lank (Bun-man from Jacob's)—the 'angashore'—lifted the end of my bed, & I thought I was going to be landed out in middle of floor. Suppressed gig-gles & titters. 'Well, that's a "gas"-search. Looking for tunnels!!' The search-party seemed conscious of their ridiculous behaviour. (They were doing what the British did more efficiently in the Tan days.) General laughter when they went out & darkness reigned again. Sleep.

12 March 1923

LICE—the prison & camp varieties. Body-lice, pubic lice (crabs—lavatories—'blue-butter') scabies—the female burrows into flesh & the male pursues her—itch—shamefacedness of men while they suffer agonies—furtive picking of shirts in quiet corners—shaking of shirts—fumigator means of propagating them—'they get fat on Keating's powder'—the Russian army fumigators (Liam Murphy of Cork: 'at the 'Kinlar (Ballykinlar)[45] we used to be plagued with sand-lice—double-bodied fellows like pismires. They'd get into your blanket.—oh, Lord! I've seen a bucketful of them, crawling mass, carried out by orderlies in the morning.')

Tuesday 20 March 1923

Lovely day. First warmth in sun. Men lying out in exercise-field watching football match between Huts 12 & 13. Walked around with Seán Kavanagh, Eamonn Enright, Judge the Philadelphian & a Dingle tailor—lame, one leg, crutch—named Houlihan. Talked of Joe McGarritty, Philadelphia, Dr. McCartan[46] etc. etc.—As we came in after tea great excitement over shooting of one of the sentries in Hare Park compound, by his comrade in a block-house. Kneeling figures of Tommies, caps off,—dying man lying wounded with bandage about temples, priest anointing him. A sentry's fire smouldering, smoke blowing across scene & kneeling figures in light air. These accidents will happen so long as these F.S. 'goups' can't keep 'one out of the spout'—constant fiddling with bolts—'Better that it should be in the oil-bottle, than in the poor devil's brain-pan!' as one of the prisoners remarked.—No confirmation of executions of Ernie O'Malley, Peadar O'Donnell & Michael Kilroy[47]. 'Whoever starts these rumours in the Camp ought to be plugged'—L. M. *dixit*.

Thursday 22 March 1923

In Hut 7 (Dining Hall) H. Francis Stuart[48] read his poems to me. Sean Kavanagh present. Cold, bare interior of tin hut—bare deal tables & forms—tables sticky & fragrant with previous day's dinner of fish. 'Munich. Autumn 1921', 'The Propylaea: Munich', 'Autumn', 'Donau' (German name of the Danube). Faint murmur of voice à la Golding & Ezra Pound. (Talked of Ezra's dressing-gown, beard, one gold earring in ear). As he read & Kavanagh & I listened, two toughs from Tralee came in—manoeuvred over like bullocks in a field to a tent, listened. We finished. Toughs awaiting courtmartial by 3 officers of line for stealing fish-boxes from No 6 cookhouse. Humorous faces. 'Do you want a counsel for defence?' 'No'—'well able to defend ourselves.' One of them commandeered a pony & trap near Tralee during scrap—wild, humorous, elemental; Sean Kavanagh, Stuart & I thought the whole scene dramatic in the extreme: Courtmartial officers had not turned up by the time we left—free & easy discipline among irregular prisoners.

Sun 25 March 1923

Prisoners (Mick Rooney) working diligently at macramé bags (ladies bags)—frame hung on posts of huts (old partition posts of cavalry stables 5th Lancers). Black & gold; blue & purple. What ideas they have, too, in the blending of colors—'a crimson silk lining would look well in that bag, sir.' Wool table-centres on frames. Ring-making out of fashion, for the time. (Claddagh crowned heart between hands: interlaced Celtic designs. 'Paudeen took my files off me & I coming into the Joy.' Murray the Boyle coachbuilder. Make a ring in a morning.)

Sun. 25 March 1923

Very cold. No smokes (altho' some of H.Q. staff are to be seen pulling at fags). Bronchitis slightly on chest—hoarse voice. Seán Kavanagh came along about 12 noon & we sat on the edge of my bed in Hut 12 talking over my 'Irregular's Diary'. Looking at the battered notebook & separate sheets on which it is written (warworn look, book taken to pieces in Mountjoy & hidden away in various 'caches' of my own to avoid capture by Paudeen. Got through search of Censors coming into Camp Tintown 2. without being detected), he said: 'That book will be in a museum one day. Gogarty, when he hears of it & when the Republic gets on top, will be coming to you recultivating your friendship.' I said: It will be like those relics of the Civil War one sees in the Smithsonian Institute in Washington—generals' active service uniforms, hats, water-bottles: it brings the stirring incidents of that stirring period—the very personalities & *persons* of the actors in it—very close to one. Anything that's intimate & first hand is of interest, humanly—anything that brings nobility, altruism, heroism near enough to ordinary mortals is of perennial interest.'

Sunday 8 April 1923 8 p.m.

Sat round fire—Liam Murphy, Seán Ó Tuama, Paddy Sullivan, Eamon Carlos of Boyle, Roscommon etc. talking about the habits of wild things. Sleeping fox on warm rock—one eye seemed to be open. A friend of Liam Murphy saw an old dog fox—or was it the vixen?—teaching two cubs how to 'forage'. Ears pricked, muzzle alert. How different it is to shoot snipe, 'the moment you've the bird sighted' (the rule in game-shooting) 'fire!' 'But with snipe,' said Carlos 'you've to wait till the bird gives 3 turns & then fire.' Story of Bill Corey knocking down the snipe with sod of turf—'but that was as the cow caught the hare—by accident.' L. Murphy story of the landlord. He was an absentee & had come to his estate with an English friend. Talking one night over drinks & smokes in library, the butler entered. 'A man wants to see you, sir. He's a brace of snipe.' Man shown in—typical peasant. Snipe accepted & glass of grog given in exchange. Exit. When he was gone the landlord remarked to his friend: 'Would you believe it? That fellow owes me 3 years rent & yet he has the audacity to come in here etc.' 'Why don't you put him out?' remarked the Englishman. 'Put him out? Have a heart. That man can shoot snipe.' (Moral was that if he could shoot snipe, he wouldn't miss a man!) Wildgeese over Ballykinlar—the 'gandal eolais' [*'Gander of knowledge'*]. Sean O'Tuama said the irregulars killed & ate several black deer at Killarney. 'The grouse is an ugly awkward bird'—'girrr—come back!' Often trapped pheasants in rabbit-traps & snares. Woodcock—lie until you put your foot on them –protective colouring. 'Drumming' of snipe in May during the hatching season—liquid sound in fine twilights—always associate sound with fine weather.—'It's a strong man will hold a brace of greyhounds on the leash'—'70 lbs of strain'. W. Donohue the famous southern 'slipper.' Cruelty of coursing—escape & trap for hares—hare doesn't be long in finding the escape—run again until killed. No sport like beating up hare out of cover of mountain & loosing the dogs on him. Stories of Roscommon curate—photographs—Bishop's injunction. ' I see you're fond of a bit o blood here.' Talk drifted to conscription & plan to meet it. Buried oatmeal. Potato-pits level with ground. Sheep on hills. Cattle—'finest of cattle in Golden Vein. As fat as stall-feds & all grass fed.' Long Walks: '*Na sléibhánaigh* [mountain dwellers].' Tramps & itineraries over hills of Wicklow in bad weather. Walk from Glendalough to top of Lugnaquillia 3039 feet. Tramps in Sean Toomeys country to West of Gougane Barra. Walk from Terenure to top of Lugnaquillia & back inside 24 hours—70 miles 'non-stop' walk.

Wednesday 11 April 1923 [BLACK DAY—Liam Lynch's Death[49].]

A fine sunny—*mild, moist*—morning after 3 or 4 days cold N. E. wind. As soon as the Hut (12) was opened & I had gone out to washhouse, Paddy Sullivan told me, 'Liam Lynch is captured—in a dying condition.' Consternation, followed by depression. Topic of conversation at breakfast in No 6 Dining Hall. (Cork men in the very depths of the 'blues' after last nights talk round No 4 stove in Hut 12. Their pessimistic talk depressed me still more—and annoyed me. I longed for the smell of clean air & wide spaces!) Seán Kavanagh came sauntering along (always with the same, slow noiseless walk, smiling sphinx-like face & hands in pockets of shabby blue slacks.) Together we went off to Hut 17 to see H. F. Stuart. Stuart gave me about a pound each of tea & sugar—most generous. 'This is a symbolic act' I said to him as I took the packets from him. After the letter (so bitter) I wrote to Nancy last night my heart thawed out. We spoke of the bad news & of the Cork men's pessimism. 'They've their sentences cut & dried already. 500 prisoners will be held & sentenced to long terms of imprisonment—5 years, 10 years. Others will be executed. A good many will be deported out of the country etc. etc.' 'Ah,' said Christy Byrne[50] irritably, 'There'll be nothing of the sort. You'll get a kick on the arse & be told to go home.' General laughter—which helped to chase away the terrible mental depression of the last few days. (I know the cause of it now. (1) No parcels or letters, annoyance with N. (2) N. E. wind, (3) Impending death of Liam Lynch & cave-in in Munster.)

RUMOUR OF CAPTURE OF DE VALERA, HUMPHRY MURPHY DAN BREEN[51] etc. 12 noon.

We went off & I had a chat with the Commdt. (E. Enright) & another officer. Was told that Lynch had died of his wounds. We spoke of the fighting in the S. & W. I remarked: 'Cork seems to have let us down badly in this scrap.' The officer who was with Enright flared up. 'Let us down!' he said. 'Not in West Cork, anyway. We were fighting 1 to 40 there.' I praised the quiet, deep, simple Russian-like Western lads (Mick Rooney, Hawkins of Loughrea, Carlos of Boyle etc.) Even that they have no education, they seem to be so right—*to have faith*—to believe implicitly in the idea of Cathleen ni Houlihan. They have such a sure contact with the realities—earth, sky, tradition. They are so extraordinarily intelligent, too—amazed me, looking at their poor clothes & shy—if splendid—presences. So different to the 'Jackeen' types of Dublin & Cork city (Peter White, Baldy Walsh—'The baldy flute stick'—Paddy Connolly). These city-bred jackeens are buoyant, boisterous, humorous, sing jazz choruses from Tivoli & Empire theatres, leaders in all noise & uproar, good hearted, unintelligent. They are not in touch with tradition—know nothing of culture etc.—Went back with Sean K. and Stuart. Irish class in Hut 7 postponed until tomorrow (Thursday). Kavanagh said a few quiet words about Liam Lynch & the big class dispersed quietly. In the wash-house (where I washed handkerchiefs) I could feel the sorrow in the men's hearts as they rubbed their shirts etc. on the boards—they emitted an aura of low-spiritedness. Dumbfoundedness. I began to lilt 'Kelly, the boy from Killann' sadly & yet triumphantly. Before I was aware others were lilting it too—a sort of subdued chorus. (It affected me like the humming of 'John Brown's Body' in Drinkwater's play 'Abraham Lincoln'). Felt such a wave of emotion surging up in my heart—tears in eyes in spite of myself—which eased the burden of my soul immensely. 'Well, they can't plug us *all*.' said a fellow to me as I went out—the cheerfulness of the remark was a tonic, after the successive waves of depression, tears etc. As I came in from military parade & rosary, was handed a letter from Nancy by Tom Rynne, Line Adjutant, dated Sunday 8.3.23. After dinner I walked with Seán Kavanagh in the mild sunshiny shelter of 15 Hut. (Outside shelter a slight nip in wind from the Wicklow Hills). Glorious clouds in sky. Wicklow Hills 20 miles off, faint grey blue colour, with gold here & there. Growth in air. Grass greener. Sheep grazing quietly beyond the barbed wire of compound. Clumps of furze beginning to break into golden blossom. The year has turned—such sweetness in air—& such *sadness*. Barbed wire & blockhouses & ugly red of barracks hideous—a blot on the beauty of the scene. Seán K's 'tavern' wreathed in blue smoke, as if they were burning something at the back. An odd racehorse out—at a walk—or an easy canter. Enright the Commdt. came along, with the doctor (Comer). The M. O. spoke of the prisoner very sick in Hospital (16 Hut)—'Brights'. 'If he dies the relatives should press for an inquest. The F. S. M. O., although informed of need of medicine, only came in when the man was in a dying condition. 'I'd no idea that he was so bad!' Of course, not. Absolute neglect of sick men—no care—no feeling. Scabies cases returned daily to huts, because no room in segregation hut in Camp 1. (Jack Staunton, & 2 others came back with their beds to Hut 12 the other day. It's a mercy if any of us escape the horrible thing). Enright made good today certainly as Commandant Enright told us in simple terms of the circumstances of L. Lynch's death. 'Army Council meeting in a farmhouse between Clonmel & Newcastle, Tipp. Sudden approach of Staters. Lynch decided to save his comrades by ambush. Deployed forces. After 2 hours fight broke cover & it was then that he got hit. De Valera, Dan Breen, Countess Markievicz[52] & *others* got away—Ruttledge[53] may have been there. Comrades tried to get Lynch away but had to leave him behind in F. S. hands. Died 8.35 last night (Tuesday). The *Independent* (wretched rag) says he was a man of outstanding personal courage & great ability! Ye Gods. These creatures not worthy to wipe his boots, I remarked: 'As you tell the story, Eamonn, it sounds like one of the great epic stories of Irish history. Hundreds of years hence that story will be told to Irish children.' We went off sad, if triumphant. Military parade of all prisoners in triangle between Huts 16 & 17 at 3 p.m. Each Hut marched out, 100 strong & stood at ease—lovely warm sun shining in sky. F.S. sentries beyond wire. Country gig with 3 men in it on road above stopped to watch. Enright gave the command 'Parade: Kneel!' All knelt down. Seán K. *stood* in middle of open triangle & recited Rosary in Gaelic; Litany of B.V.M. Subdued, earnest responses. Marched back again. After lock-up there was an 'identification parade'. 47 F. Staters came at slow march along prisoners 'standing to beds'—a vile looking C.I.D. stranger in green collar & snooker cap, shaven upper lip—peered sharply into each man's face. When gone prisoners look from one to other & ask 'What's it for?' To bed—depressed.

Mon 23 April

A time of trouble begins. First news as I talked to F. Stuart 2-30 p.m. G. Wallace 'O/C arrested.' Went out afterwards & Seán Mooney told me at latrine that the trouble was over names of O/C's of huts. Told P–W–[Peter White] who took the thing half humorously & wholly seriously. Before tea P. W. told men that he was O/C no longer & that men could stand to beds or not as they wished. About 11.30 p.m. (sleeping with one eye open) we heard the pulling of beds & banging in other huts. Thought at first it was prisoners in huts 11 & 13 beginning 'obstruction' policy. About 12-15 a.m. (Tuesday morning) enter Dep. 'Bunny', red sergeant etc. etc. (about 8 or 10 of them) with guns. Went round beds pulling them out from wall. Pulled down boxes & dressers. Took coal buckets, tables, pokers, BRUSHES etc. General relief when they went off—laughter—jokes. 'Mind your head'—box thrown. Very tired—did not sleep for a long time. Siege anticipated. Tea. Loaves. Water. Buckshee coal from washhouse. 'Probably [illegible] last time' said P.J.

Tuesday 24 April 1923

Nobody got up. Beautiful sunshiny warm morning shining thro' windows. Doors locked. ROTTEN SMELL from bucket—leaking—mopped up—Bacilikil. Carlos got out to try to get a bucket of coal & L. M.'s box etc. Skedaddled back as two P. A. men were in wash-house.—'Get back!' Made tea on stove 4. No count. No letting out to breakfast. About 2 doors opened & men let out (as they thought to latrines) carts rolling along laden with tables, boxes, beds etc. Driven down to compound. Dep. with cane & revolver & sinister group near clothes rails. 'Ooze off to the compound.' Men herded down like sheep by P. A.'s could see huts being searched by search party of P. A.'s. Got overcast & very cold wind (from S.) about 3 p.m. Men gathered (like bees) in groups. Scattered. Reformed. Man digging tunnel for joke surrounded by others. Beds being carried out of huts by search parties. 'They're taking out the beds now.' 'All the utensils are being taken out.' About 4 p.m. F–S– [*Frank Stuart*] directed my attention to Bunny hanging out of the end window of 18 Hut & calling to comrades (Dep. & other officers & P. A.'s standing in sinister group at head of rails where clothes are dried.) Tunnel in 18 discovered. Went all day on mug of tea & piece of bread & butter with sugar.

Rumour tunnel in Hut 1 discovered. Men moving about sullenly & aimlessly. Walking to keep themselves warm. Behan said: 'The darkest hour's before dawn. They wouldn't put sheep in a pen this way.' 'They'd give them a bite of hay anyway.' Men lying in great crowd on concrete—taking up places for the night. Men of Maryboro' prepared with overcoats etc. Man in stocking soles. Man in shirtsleeves from washhouse, with towel for turban. Cheery, tragic groups & salutations—Fr. Daly, Barney Walsh, P. Sullivan, Carlos, Hawkins, P.J. Ryan etc. Tom Rynne. 'We'll be out all night.' Men dejected & leg-weary. Shot fired from '45 (Dep) beyond wires. 'Zizz-z-z-z' over our heads—heavy calibred bullet. 'How, how, how.' Men all in hollows of compound by 5 p.m. Very cold. Men will faint—20 cases at Maryboro'. Men blue—kidneys caught. 9.10 p.m. ordered into line (non-military formation) by red sergeant & filed past Dep & others for count & scrutiny. Rushed then at double to latrines & into huts. (Huts 1 & 18 closed, 'any man going near them will be shot'). Into Hut 12. Dull electric light—miserable-looking. Blankets, papers, boxes etc. etc. in litter over floors—very dirty. NO CHANCE OF WASHING—LATRINE buckets containing excrement & full of urine unemptied. Lit fire of old boxes etc. Voice of P.A. outside 'Put out that fire.' Enter Dep. & Bunny. 'Get into your beds or get out.' My can of water on fire: took it off. 'You'll get nothing. You'll get what you deserve. F—you!' Exit Dep. with cane. Bunny knocked over two mugs with end of revolver. Enter P.A. with Jeyes fluid water can & puts out fire. Into bed without food, very tired. Several raids for count during night. Scrutiny of faces under blankets. Guns. As P.A. man got to end of hut 12 light switched off. 'Turn on light.' 'It's switched off.' 'Oh, glory be to Jesus'—laugh—exit. Fell asleep very tired—glad to be alive after a most trying & eventful day. Sheehan told me that a lot of my stuff was in his box. Is my shaving kit gone? Saved journal.

[*Notes*]

We'll be falling out of our standing by dark—7 hours.

Suggested Tom Rynne say the Rosary—tried to find adjutant Regan in crowd, but failed. Too cold to say the Rosary.

Gannon caught by skirt of breeches & hung over the wires.

[Prisoners were made to dig a trench around the camp. This was objected to as forced labour.]

Fri. 27 April 1923

Slept very little from 2 a.m.—the result of yesterday's strain. Heard a traction engine going—also a goods train panting along slowly on the G.S.W. line. (no 1 post & all's well No 2 etc. No 3 does not answer & repetition.) Dreams—half decided to make a protest against forced labour—but don't want to 'make a Robert Emmet of myself' as the prisoners keep saying. Kept thinking of the beatings with revolver butts & agonising yells in Hut 13 & outside it later. Much the same feeling of strain as in the 'Joy after 10th Oct 1922 & 8th Dec. 1922. Poor old heart reeling in its action. Sun arose about 6—heard drip-drip of white frost from galvanised roof. Also tap-tap of water-drops on piece of tin or iron in gully outside. Crows & seagulls very lively as they always are on a sunny morning. Damnable bugle reveillé—hatefullest of sounds. Reminiscences of the 'Joy. (A good deal of firing all the night.) L. M. awakened & poked Paddy S. 'Paddy! Paddy!'—no reply. Then Paddy awakes & looks sharply at watch & says it's [½] seven. Paddy's laugh not heard now—humorous men easily depressed L. M. says he's heard picks & shovels all morning—but picks & shovels are on everybody's brain. Dream that P.A. man came in to me in dark & offered to let me escape: 'You won't betray me?' I said, doubtingly. It's so hard to keep sane & cool & hopeful at a time like this. A P. A. begins to rattle a stone or stick along the corrugations of the huts—horrible racket. Kicks at door of 12. Then the rattle-rattle of corrugations again—a sort of fife & drum band tattoo. Goes along to spyhole in door at side of my bed—face looks in. An old tin (condensed milk) set on edge of spyhole—thought it was a gun at first. The P. A. shouts something in & gives the tin a knock with muzzle of gun & it shoots in to Hut 12 at stove 4. (With the muzzle of the gun he was making the racket along corrugations). 'They're in No 11 now.' Everybody up & dressed. Some go back, in clothes, to bed to await entry of Counters. Usual entry—tall thin P. A. (he carries his gun in his pocket & is *not too* bossy). Then R–S–[*Red Sergeant*] 'Stand properly at ease everywhere' (nudgings & looks of prisoners). Bunny & Slinky & others. R–S– says to P. Hogan 'Come on, boy' ditto to Corky R. The guns are in hands, but not so truculently drawn as yesterday & day before. Aura of hate not so perceptible. Bunny's teeth & trench coat, grey cap & leggings—stableman all over. Slinky can't lift head off ground. Peering round for tunnel openings. As they go out of door B. turns round & calls out '1583 regarding release'. No reply. Repeats number. Corky responds 'Socko' in a loud voice. General laughter & disapproval of Corky's exclamation. 'We'll be surely on the labour shift today.': Men discuss their prowess, or lack of it, with picks & shovels. 'We'll see what Carlos can do now in a boghole.' Called out for breakfast 9.30. a.m. Dining Hall 6 very dirty—tables like pig troughs—no brushes, no orderlies. 'Clear out now & let the others in!' from P. A. (ex Red-Cap) in very Cockney accent. 'Thank the Lord it's not a Cork accent' loq. L. M. Rush for latrines—queue waiting to get in. Hurry skurry out. P. A.'s firm, but not unfriendly. In wash-house:– 'Get in lads. Here's the B's & T's' (i.e. the Smith Wesson brigade) Hut 12 very dirty—unswept since Monday morning. Latrine buckets oozing over channels of stables. General hurry to get them emptied & clean water in. Shave myself & *wash* in my mug—unwashed since Tuesday. P. W. strips to waist & washes himself in bath. Horseplay etc. 'murder gang.' Shot from '45—10.15 a.m. Stack & another hammered yesterday back in Camp—'muscles of arm round to the front.' Has signed the form—don't wonder. Easy to blame him. Men fooling about in good spirits. Shouts. Whistles. Laughs. Chess. Cards. Macramé bags. Strangers from Hut 18 marching up & down. Strained & tense. Heart weak. Settle down on wires of bed to read *La Vie d'Un Simple*. As the sun is shining outside & there is so much noise it is hard to concentrate on the book. The horseplay & foolish laughter irk me—part of the punishment of being a prisoner. Mick Dowd of Delgany wanders over to my bed, stands about, says nothing, kicks one heel against the other, hands in pockets, says only: 'Ach, it's a hard ould life'—&, as I do not reply, drifts away to a group of friends from Tallaght on the other side of hut. Imprisonment is very hard on a man like this, I fancy.—10.30 a.m. A sudden crying in Hut 11. Everybody silent. Hush!-h-h! Then after a silence in which a pin could be heard dropping: It's only tricking. He says: 'Come out & fight.' Resumption of noise.

2 p.m. Called out for dinner. Outside Dining Hall 7 saw Stack surrounded by a crowd of prisoners—white face, gold glasses, teeth on one side of upper jaw missing. His coat punctured & ripped, back, front & sleeves with bayonets yesterday. Face unmarked. Tea 5 p.m. first time since Monday to have 3 meals. Peter W. ate his tea off the altar-table—mocking of No. 4 section. Dining Hall floor filthy—covered with potato skins etc. Suppose it will be swept up at point of gun—if brushes are supplied. At tea heard rumours (1) P.M. General killed in ambush somewhere in Mayo (2) 2 men shot, 2 bayonetted in Hare Park Camp (3) escape of prisoners from Gormanstown[54]. Shut in, after getting bath & tea-bucket full of clean water from taps of washhouse. Count 6 p.m. Not so many gunmen on the job (before being shut in saw Ned Hegarty, worried-looking). F. Stuart came in & said that Hut 17 was having the devil of a time. Another raid—belongings knocked about—faces of prisoners facing away from hut outside & told not to look round. Hut 17 congested with men from Hut 18—'very uncomfortable,' 'two in a bed', said Stuart with his boyish smile. Ryder said, 'We're getting the treatment of blacks'. Several Hut 17 men (18 men) taken out on digging trench. 7 p.m. broad daylight. Shinners (?) leaning out of window at end of hut talking across to somebody in Hut 11. A violin begins to play *The Coulin*—general stoppage of noise. Then *The Marseillaise*—everybody whistles the refrain. Merry, but strained feeling in the air—war not yet over, nor like to be.

Friday 4 May 1923

9 p.m. I feel warm & fed after porridge (given me from No. 2 stove by Connie Ryan) and tea. As I passed down the hut from the only fire burning (No 2) with my little salmon-can of tea Charley MacDonagh said: 'It's a hard ould life, Mr. Campbell.' I sit on my bed, just made

down for the night, and write this. Long May twilight & sun streaming thro' windows. Very warm. Murmur of talk & laughter in the hut. P.J. Ryan has been reading Larkin's speech on his return to Dublin after 8 years from Tuesday's (1st. May) paper. Group listening to him. Song starts: 'Glory O! Glory O! for the bold Fenian men,' with chorus. Since count we have been expecting a shift. The devil's game of musical chairs is being played with the prisoners from hut to hut. No 17 were shifted yesterday evening (tramp-tramp on hollow-sounding ground past our windows about 7.p.m) to No 1. No 5, it seems, went to No 2 this evening. To add to the strain & tension (which has been almost intolerable) of the past 8 days we have the uncertainty of a shift any evening hour. One's heart leaps & reels at the sound made by the old wooden bar shutting the door. The bar creaks & bangs; then enter the Huns—'What are they up to now?' We live on the edge of an earthquake. Then there is the daily passing of the escort with shining bayonets to lead off the forced labour gang to the trench-digging. As we were at breakfast this morning we saw the bayonets passing the windows of No 6 Dining Hall & then the poor commandeered ones being led off with picks & shovels. Galley-slavery—absolutely illegal. The tension in one's heart & nerves is extreme, & all the prisoners show the effects of it. Fr. Stuart's story of Fr. Garland's behaviour on his removal from 17 to 1 hut. He thought it was release, at first, & showed unbounded delight. Then when he got to No 1 he went momentarily off his head & began pulling out the beds, one after the other. Insanity in family: domestic worries—only married a week when arrested & wife left him. No account of her. Sheets being taken from prisoners. Men get other prisoners' blankets—dirty—venereal disease. What cares the F. S?—This morning about 1 a.m. two P. A. men entered & as they came past my bed they saw coal emptied at the door. 'Buckshee coal from the cook-house!' (It was from the washhouse, as a matter of fact). The sergeant drew his gun & covered J.J. Walsh in bed. 'I'll give you 10 seconds to get that f–ing coal humped out of that.' J. jumped out & said ' I've nothing to do with it.' 'I know you haven't.' Shovelled the wet coal & slack with bare hands into porridge basin, covering up wooden spoon. 'What'll I do with it?' said the P. A., unwillingly lifting it. 'Oh, dump it on a bed!' Exeunt in darkness. The incident was a comic one, even though a gun was drawn menacingly. Laughter. 'Oh, talk about it in the morning,' said George Wallace. Sleep.

Sun. 6 May 1923

After count 8 a.m. B. announces 'out to the washhouse to wash & all men return to hut.' Door locked 8.10 a.m. Paraded for Mass. I didn't move. B. comes along. 'Are you an R.C., Mac?' I replied: 'I hope there's freedom of conscience where religion is concerned'. 'Oh, it's all right.' 'Thanks' I reply. Steve Hastings, the Larkinite (come in yesterday to our hut with 5 others) does not go either. I have a bath (only *one* official bath in 3 months in Tintown) by my bedside. He sits on J.J. Walsh's bed & talks. 'Larkin's strike—the Countess[55] Dev's whore—chance of a worker's republic, what will Jim Larkin do?' (Larkin on the brain.) Walked around compound with Joe Judge & Paddy Houlihan of Dingle. Met old Keogh & another. Lie down on (dampish) grass. K talks of Galveston Texas—ranche—depressing life of cowpunchers—not a bit like the pictures—Argentina—Rosario—Bulfin—Southern Cross[56] etc. Larry Ginnell's[57] black hat with the rhythm in the brim.

[Campbell was taken ill with flu in May, and moved to the Hospital Hut. The following entries for June all refer to this period of his hospitalization.

Outside, Frank Aiken, Republican Chief of Staff issued a cease-fire order on 24 May 1923.]

Sunday 3 June 1923

Still in bed, but feeling much better. That queerish, unnatural feeling that accompanies 'flu—something that doesn't belong to one—gone for the most part. Coolish grey morning, as men assemble outside for Mass in Hut 17. Camp returning to normal after the dreadful happenings since 24 April. No guns; no intimidation. After dinner the usual crowd of visitors came in. Several men in to see the poor young Kerryman (sore abscessed lip, due to bad blood) next to me since Dick

Sinnott's departure on Saturday afternoon. Like Job I'm living now with what my soul abhors; Coughing; spitting or rather hawking; & all the signs of disease to which poor mortality is subject. *War & Peace* atmosphere. Fr. Stuart came along & we talked, as usual, on literary matters—the Tennyson article in the *Times* Supplt. of April 12th 23. How hard it is to appraise one's contemporaries. Talked of the boosting of authors that goes on in the *Times*—Austin Clark's praise of Rolleston? Old C.K. Shorter Lity. letter in Sphere—Louise Imogen Guiney.[58] CKS. likes & dislikes—his falling foul of Edmund Gosse. Borrow's originality, Samuel Butler; Herman Melville—originality taboo. Hardy's poems—how good they are. Have never read The Dynasts. Seán K. came along—looking very American in blue serge, double-breasted coat etc. Sean's great head—black hair, bullet cranium, character—and yet what is wrong with him? Seán held forth in a torrent of eloquence, with gesture & mobile face—pessimism. We talk of our loyalty. Liam Lynch trapped in a farmhouse in spite of his guard; Austin Stack captured in a potato-field; Denny Lacy killed; Roger Casement etc.[59] 'How many of you fellows' (crowd had gathered to listen to him) 'were got in a farm-house taking tea? And you talk of soldiers! Why God damn it man, I travelled 4000 miles to fight—and for what? We had Limerick & we ran away. We had Bruree & we gave it up to a pack of bastards. At Kilmallock[60] I was ordered about by a fellow thatched with notes he had looted from a bank. I saw one Irregular with 3 guns on him, a Peter on his leg, another, a 45 in his pocket; a rifle in his hand & two bandoliers of ammunition—about a thousand rounds, & yet we ran away. One O/C came along & said the defences were splendid, another came along half an hour later & said: "They're rotten. The windows want to be sandbagged." I said to him: "To sandbag these windows you want two things—bags & sand—neither of which we've got. Will you tell us where we're going to get them." ' I laughed & suggested—blankets, sheets (as in Hut 18 in the tunnel) & the earth about—but Seán was too full of *his saeva indignatio* [savage indignation] to listen. Eventually his dark face broke into a wreath of smiles & he said 'We're a great race, no mistake'.

Mon. 4 June 1923

Rumour of shift of prisoners to Newbridge 1, 2 & 3 huts. Fr. Stuart, with his pleasant smile, bade me goodbye on the strength of it 5.30 p.m. 'will see Seán (MacBride)[61] there.'

P.J. Ryan came in today about 11 a.m., grave & bearded & had a long conversation with me. He is now Camp Adjt. Trouble in camp over order to Hut O/C's to line up their men for trench-work. They say that propaganda will be made out of it by F. S. outside. They will say that we are working voluntarily under our own officers. Peter White in Hut 12 would resign rather than march his hut up to gate to be handed over to F. S. officers for forced labour. A point to be considered. There was a debate—& grave difference of opinion on it—in the huts last night. Rumour of a strike of cookhouse staff over dismissal of Q. M. Shall we ever have peace in the Camp? We are a queer race; but Camp & gaol life is not a criterion to judge anybody by. Men of different tastes, temperaments & degrees of education lumped together—unable to get away from each other—with division deliberately fomented by the enemy—jealousies between would-be leaders eaten up with an idea of their own importance—bound to come up against each other. Breakdown of *morale*, too, of a militarily-beaten army. We got on to the subject of release. Dick Mulcahy is a pale, thin-lipped, merciless type of individual, capable of the utmost refinement of torture. He is quite capable of talking as he was reported to talk in Monday's paper re rapid release of prisoners, simply to raise their hopes with the ultimate object of dashing them! I told him of Dick Sinnott's impression in the Ryans house near Wexford.[62] A naturally taciturn individual, given to sporadic—if rare—bursts of alleged humour. His face a sour, humourless face—misanthropic, cynical. And yet he can, as you know, rise at times to a kind of flight of perverted idealism (as in his speech in the Abbey Theatre on the failure of the poets in the Tan War) and in his speech at the graveside at Collins' funeral.

Got up after dinner—first time for over 3 weeks. Very groggy on legs & giddy in head. Sat around stove after count talking with the other convalescents. Big tin dixie boiling. To bed 9 p.m. As I lay awake Dr.

Comer put the Evening Telegraph under my pillow. Robbery from Boland's Mill of £1375 by two young men with guns—one in uniform of National Army! Protectors of property! The demobbed men will get rich quickly, no mistake.

9 p.m. Group of orderlies & convalescents round table copying from heap of autograph books brought to me by prisoners.

I wish I were a golden ring
Upon a fair maid's hand
That every time she loosed her blouse
I could see her—you understand.

Sniggers & laughs. Concert over blanket curtain.

Sun 10 June 1923

Cool, windy morning. Bad unseasonable weather still continues. After Mass Dr Comer came over to me & said, 'The F. S. M. O. has a bad a/c of Dr. Fearon. Dying at 7 o'clock last evening. Mother & wife sent for. It will be providential if he pulls through.' I said that if he died it would stop the idiotic mockery about 'amenities in prisons.' The hardship of his previous terms in jail telling on him now. The constitution of a horse would break down under it. The fact that the Local Govt. Ministry under sealed order deprived him of the M/O ship of Swinford district told on a sensitive man, no doubt. Little provision for wife & children as he was a man that gave no thought to money & attended the poor free in big areas of Connacht. L. G. Ministry's action mean & contemptible—no thought for previous services to Nation, or for wife & small children of a man who remained faithful to his oath as a Republican.

Informed later that B.—had rounded up two or 3 men in compound who were not at Mass & ran them up outside the 'gate', where they were compelled to remain without breakfast or dinner. Freedom of conscience—Christian charity!

Fr. Stuart—tall, deprecating, smiling—in after dinner. Big crowd of visitors sitting round prisoners' beds. Animation & friendly chat. Frank returned me copies of N. Y. Freeman & N. Y. Times Lity Supplement of April 29 1923 which I had lent him. He liked an article on Paul Morand: 'Paul Morand's colourful Gallery of Fiction Portraits'—reviews of his books: *Ouvert la Nuit* (1922) and *Fermé la Nuit* (1923). Quote. Cosmopolitanism & wide sweep of American literary papers. Paddy Houlihan came along with his crutch & sat down on bedside. When I told him that my wife had seen J–E– he was all attention & inquisitiveness (of a naive kind). 'Great man, J–. I knew he could do his work well'. Seán a Chóta came along, pink, smiling, dark, shaven, in blue p. coat & withered Paddy with a sarcastic look. 'God damn it all,—great man! We have no great men in this country. Nobody "with sand"—not one. Not enough brains in the country to run a shit-house. Somebody in the Hut (5) last night talked about still having the flag. What flag? said I. Haven't the Staters appropriated it?' Then he sighed a deep breath & shrugged his square shoulders violently—and smiled broadly. Mick Rooney came along—Fred Hawkins—Paddy Sullivan & sat on Liam Murphy's bedside. Talk, talk—then Leo's imperative command: 'Time up. All visitors out!' Tea—egg. Got up & shaved. Must obey N's [*Nancy's*] injunction about not growing a beard. Before going away I called Seán K & told him that I had got into trouble with a woman. Had told Frank Stuart to pull Seán's leg about it. Seán very concerned. Told Seán to pull Frank's leg about it in turn. The poet's privilege. Lord Byron. Even the pharasaic Wordsworth and Annette Vallon (see N. Y. Times Supplt. 29 April 1923). Got yesterday's paper from Billy Walsh (quote extracts) Dick Mulcahy & cultural mission of F. S. Army. ye Gods! (quote) Talk round stove 9 p.m. after count. No crops—no meadows owing to cold & frost of mornings. Harsh ungrateful wind, Corn redding in fields. Turnips & mangolds fail to strike. Farm-labourers strike in Co. Waterford. Famine & pestilence on the top of war. Dr Comer *dixit*: 'A people that wouldn't fight deserve it all. The reward of slavery. We're a slave race & we deserve all we get. God's curse is on the damned country.' Liam Shortes came along & said that Moran's temperature was 102.8. 'A shot of strychnine before he goes to sleep.' Leo's voice:—'Get your beds made down—& get into them!'

Monday 30 July 23

I write this after Rosary (in Gaelic) said by Muirís Breathnach of Listowel. The days are shortening in. A wild gleamy sunset—yellow—through windows after showery day. Cool. Latrine bucket in position for the night; Paul Shinners pissing into it. Fires lighted under beds for supper. L. Murphy, P. Sullivan & others are working feverishly on their bed at the Turkey wool mat which they hope to complete before release. Confused talk, shuffling, crackling of sticks, clanking of buckets, sound of pissing.—The first story brought in on the doors being opened this morning after Count was—the corner of trench at blockhouse angle coming from Camp 1 direction had fallen in after last evening's torrential rain. Prayers that the blockhouse would come with it. 'No 3 post & all's well! No 3 post &—all's up', said P. Sullivan, the tailor, laughing his infectious laugh. Then the Tintown Herald Reporter—Jim Stapleton (describe his butcherish appearance—a Howth gun-runner) came in, 'All the women prisoners were released on Saturday!' I disbelieved it: too good to be true; but if so, we may expect release soon. 'Hats off to the ladies!' Then another rumour afloat: 'No prisoners to be released until after the elections.'—Did not believe either. As I wrote last night in my letter to N. [*Nancy*]: 'I have ceased to look on optimism as a virtue.' Seán K. in after breakfast. Told me what he wrote in his Gaelic diary last night. 'The torrential flood of rain. Quiet that fell on the hut as the prisoners listened to the deluge on tin roof of 5 Hut. Heard his American watch ticking under his pillow. Snore of a prisoner on his bed asleep. Farts from another man asleep.' How queer a thing, how primitive a thing is humanity!—After dinner, news of the day's paper from Cookhouse 6. Meeting in Sligo, Sunday, not a F. S. success. The Revd. Chairman disappointed at lack of interest in new-found freedom.—Fr. Fagan of Columbus, Ohio, at O Connell St. prisoners' meeting said that Ireland had two enemies—John Bull and the Irish Bishops. I said: 'She has three—J.B., the Bishops & the Irish people themselves.'—Since I ate Norah's[63] French sardines I have been troubled with a sense of a belly on me. Must take more exercise. Went off looking for a handball in Hut 17—from Cap.

Nolan. The Cap. was out. Groups of Western men—Martin O'Regan of Loughrea, O'Flaherty of Spiddal (in bed), ring-makers—fine view from open back door over sunny compound (between heavy showers), prisoners promenading—gloomy blue Wicklow hills with green patches, banks of deep violet & white huddled cloud over Lugnacullia. Deep violet threatening bank to West. Fell in with Nolan. Relate his history. How Seán K. took compassion on him in Hut 1 when he first came in—ragged beaten look, eyes protruding from head—Bunny—attitude of prisoners in hut (tunnel was going on at the time & they were suspicious of him)—introduction to Behan, a Kildare man. His treatment in Glasshouse. Threatened with torture for not divulging whereabouts of Plunket's column.[64] Régime of the glasshouse. Grocer's asst. Arrest behind counter in Maddenstown Tavern. Servant girl upstairs making beds. No possibility of employment on release. Seán K's plan—mule, cart—go round selling things.

Seán's storyish mood. Reminds him (mule, cart, tarpaulin) of a night he spent with swingboat folk in Dingle. Slept the night with the proprietor & his wife—in the one bed. Several drinks before turning into the caravan. Thought he might have a bunk to himself—but no—the wife got in first (the men pissed off the platform into the night, outside) then her husband, then Seán! Seán's Bohemianism. Gipsies of New Hampshire, Conn. Mexican-looking men with knives in their belts. No communism with women there!—Frank Stuart in with the first number (June) of 'The Adelphi'. Striking photograph of Katherine Mansfield. Beautiful head—bobbed hair—striking, seeing eyes set wide apart—passionate (rather coarse) mouth. Was she married to M. Murray? (I am in love with a Dead Woman—Cytherea is in those brooding eyes). Before count Seumas Henry of Foxford came up & sat on my bed talking. I like these fine Western men. We talked of Seán MacEoin[65] & his serving of Mass on the Reek (Croagh Patrick) yesterday, as chronicled in today's paper. The blasphemy of it. How he shot poor Mullen[66] of Mayo in Custume Barracks (Lawler fired the gun that killed him, but MacEoin was behind it). I told him I had seen MacEoin's signature pasted into an autograph book:—'Seán MacEoin Commdt. of Ballynalee.' The depths to which has sunk in Ireland. I told my wife yesterday in a letter that I had left the Catholic Church. Hate its scroungerism & materialism. Henry said that when coming from Athlone to the 'Joy, one of his escort was a fellow he had arrested in 1922—trucetime—for robbing a bank at Swinford. £5000 stolen. £4000 recovered. The search at night. The peasant house—very dirty—of 2 rooms. The old mother. The barrel of poteen 'down'. The two sons—wild men. The journey across the fields to the stone wall—rolls of notes & bags of silver. The arrest of the sons—the wailing of the old woman in the darkness. The bank gave us £250 for our trouble, but we more than spent it on expenses of removal by rail etc. to Sligo & court etc. I see the case is in the F. S. Courts now after so long an interval. 'Will we be called as witnesses & what will our attitude be to the Court?'—10 p.m. I finish this by candlelight (candle stuck on iron bedpost, given me by Paddy Clear of Foley St.) Time was, in the 'Joy, when a candle found on you would have meant B. Basement & solitary confinement & perhaps a beating. How surging my brain is with pictures of prisoners—incidents—thoughts. Life is extraordinarily colorful even inside the wires of a camp.

[9 August 1923. A revision, from notes.]

5.30 p.m.

I am sitting on my bed writing these notes. I see the poor mad prisoner known as 'Siki'[67] come slowly down the hut from the front door. He is in his bare feet. Over the right shoulder he carries his bedstead, over the left a bundle of bedding, with tin mug & plate knotted into the dirty sheet. A strong, bowed, terribly pathetic figure. He unburthens himself of his impedimenta. Without saying a word he pulls apart the beds occupied by Paddy Hogan of Scariff and 'President' Cosgrave & shoves his own into the narrow space between. My heart sinks. I know he wants to be near me because of the human kindnesses I have done him from time to time. Proximity to a lunatic in daylight is not a pleasant sensation—but what of the night? George Wallace is on J. J. Walsh's bed, scraping industriously with a penknife at his bone harp. He looks up, smiles, and nods across to me. Then he gives a broad wink towards

Jack White who lies stretched on his bed against the lower gable, the peak of his cap tilted over his gold spectacles, reading a newspaper. George is a wiseacre, and his judgment of any situation is sure to be pretty accurate. 'Trouble for Hut 12, trouble for *you*, Sir!' his nod seems to say. Quietly, sadly, 'Siki' divests himself of trousers & shirt, & with only a scanty singlet covering his strong man's nakedness, gets into bed. What will Hogan & the 'President' say when they return to find a mad man between them?

7 p.m.

The men are 'standing to their beds' for evening count. Siki gets up, and stands, self-consciously, with lowered head, in his place facing me. Hogan and Cosgrave have not yet tumbled to the situation, and are bewildered somewhat by the newcomer's presence. In his short singlet—through which his heavy pectoral muscle swells like a woman's breast—he looks like some poor zany out of a travelling show. Two uniformed Free State Officers march down the hut in step on either side, cross at the lower end, march up again, counting us quickly. The 'dismiss' is given, and the doors are barred for the night. It is not yet night; the setting sun shines with a golden-luminous glow through the western windows touching the prisoners' faces, the shirts, socks and towels festooned between the wooden uprights with beauty. But it is night in our hearts.

8.35 p.m.

There is considerable commotion without. The men of Huts 10 and 11 are being paraded in 'Fifth Avenue.' Something unusual is happening. 'What can it mean?' J. J. Walsh asks me. 'Release?' 'Release, my hat!' snaps George Wallace. "Siki" has put the wind up the Staters. The count is out. They think somebody has escaped.' George is right; the official tally of the 1,500 odd prisoners in the camp does not square. The bar on the front door goes up. Enter 'Bunny' Lynam and Reilly, keen as bloodhounds, both in civilian rig—tweed caps, blue jackets, breeches and leggings. Raising his cane, 'Bunny' shouts peremptorily: 'All out for roll-call!' A prisoner's life is not a happy one, but it has its compensations. It is fine to see the twilight sky, and to taste the cool, sweet air of late summer darkfall. For over twenty minutes we are kept standing outside the hut. The ranks are broken continually; there is much craning of necks & talk—and Stephen Hastings and Paddy Lawler are well to the fore with their ribald jokes, as they always are in time of earthquake. 'Siki', I notice, is not of our company. He has ignored the order, and remains in bed. I am personally anxious, as in my precipitate exit I had to push the leaf containing these notes under my blankets. In the event of a search it might be discovered. I have a letter there, too, to N., addressed and stamped, ready to go out by the secret post Sean a' chota has maintained for so long under the nose of the Governor. Serious, if it was found.

After considerable delay poor 'Siki' appears, followed by the two sleuths. They have run their quarry to earth. He has pulled his trousers on, but his feet are still bare, and as he comes through the door-space, shouldering his awkward burden, I feel the tears filling my eyes. In the semi-darkness now he is anything but the zany, he is Christ on the way to Calvary. Slowly, silently, without demur or protest, he passes towards Hut 8, where he belongs. 'More evictions in Ireland!' someone shouts down the ranks. It is Connie Ryan's voice—Tipperary, as usual, daring and irrepressible. The uniformed officers who had already counted us come along & call out our numbers. '9130'—that is mine. '*Annso!*' ['Here']' I casually answer, and file back into the stale air & semi-gloom of the hut. My notes and letter are safe. Supper of bread & cocoa. Sleep ... I hope.

21 August 1923

Heavy rain all night. Floor of Hut 12 wet about my bed & sticky with mud. Thoroughfare by way of back door. When door was opened in morning—grey, cold, desolate. Wet shirts flapping in wind. Very few in wash-house. No faces washed on a wet morning—oh, like Job I could curse the day I was born! I understand books like 'Job', 'Timon of Athens', 'Lear', 'De Profundis'—'The Inferno', Dostoevsky's novels—as I never understood before. They have all sprung out of a terrible personal suffering. No parcel from N. No message of any kind as she promised in her letter of 14th. No remembrance from Norah. Depression an agony—heart fluttering painfully—reels in brain—sickness along the nerves & muscles of arms & legs. Is there compensation for passion? Will good or bad come out of this? Curses on the world! Curses on Destiny!—Cold, squally, heavy showers—with breaks of cool sunshine between. In sun, big, piled, white clouds in a blue sky—then sudden darkness, & the big drops begin to fall—then torrential rain.—Workmen working at concrete gutters round latrine opposite Hut 8. Does it mean long imprisonment? or, simply, finishing off a long-delayed contract. P. Houlihan after breakfast directed my attention to one of the men. 'He's a friendly fellow that. I know by the way he smiled at me. He thinks a wonder of a cripple being in. That fellow stooping down, with the shovel in his hand, & the cap on the big head'—Prisoners restless. Electionitis. P. Houlihan thin & sad—tears in eyes—sadness even in his walk & laugh. Much talk in Hut 5 of election & Republican prospects. 'God damn you & Mary MacSwiney!'[68] shouted Seán Kavanagh. 'We wouldn't recognise the Republic ourselves & we expected other countries—America—to do so. They won't let you sleep at night with their talk. I've been in this business for 20 years & I know the types. Brains? None, by Christ.'—Owing to risk of raids etc. I gave MS to Liam MacD again. As I crossed over B–y [*Bunny*] & R–y [*Reilly*] & a P. A. were standing with their backs to Hut 13. What goes on in spite of, & unknown, to them. Gave a letter to N. & Mrs. Montgomery[69] to Tom L—[*Longmore*] to post. Seán K. is worried about the '*Seana-bhouchaill*' ['old boy'][70]. 'Wouldn't like to see the poor old man come to any harm. He did well by us. If only he'd remained on for a day or two longer we'd have been able to get D–s [*Diaries*] out.'

After dinner Seán K. directed my attention to groups of prisoners down alleyway between Huts 6 & 5—hanging about inside gate at Cookhouse, all looking one way. 'They're all haunting the gate these days. They've got release on the brain. There's a fellow in Hut 3—violent dementia. He has to be handcuffed by P. A.'s at night.'—Read day's paper: showed Fr. Stuart, who came along, Cosgrave's reference to the 'Three Graces.'[71] Frank's face as he read it—indignation all over it.

Cosgrave's attacks on women—his hatred of Mme MacBride. Looked at pictures in N. Y. Times. They've an unsettling effect. So much freedom, life & luxury outside; so little inside. *No* women here. The beautiful wining, dining world, well-dressed. Our lot—same old grub, rags, etc. etc.—Parcel in 3 p.m. Note round cigarettes from N. Disappointed at its coldness. Irritable & cross. Paddy Clear came in & asked me for ink. I was bending over bed & he caught me round the waist (hate to be caught so!). 'I've no ink,' I said snappily. Paddy couldn't understand. Then I *relented*. 'Billy Walsh or J.J. Flanagan may have some.'—Round compound with Seán K. told him of my 'crossness'. 'No wonder', he said. 'Think of it. We're stalled in cavalry sheds; on a fine day we're let loose to graze in compound.' 'If only I had a steak & lobster salad—and wine! If we'd a 5£ note in our pockets what a tuck-in we'd have together on our release.' Bed down early. Wintry, dark evening. Lots of rain to fall. Bad hay-weather at home.—10 p.m. Looked out thro' spyhole in back door. Darkness. Rain falling. Ghosts of shirts flapping in melancholy wind. Lighted windows of Hut 13 opposite. Door of Hut 5 barred & silent. No P. A.'s about. As sad a night-piece as ever eye looked on. Grey roofs of huts with electric wires on standards & insulators overhead.

[A General Election was held on 27 August 1923.]

Wed. 29 August 1923

Persistently wet day.

Kelly P.A.:—'We've the keys of the f–ing gate yet'.

Drip, Drip from roof. Backdoor trouble. Wind from NE. Channels of Stable 12 flooded. Door wired up. 60 prisoners in from Galway—pitiable condition—always moved on a bad day.

Ceased about 6 p.m. Over to cookhouse. Paper from C. Byrne. Read it out to prisoners. Types. Excited faces. Grady. Seán a chóta (John of the Quota) cheers.

Republican barometer rising.

Thursday 30 August 1923

Bright sunshine, but cold. Goodly news! Goodly news said S. K. as he beckoned to me with morning's paper. Into Hut 5 where he read it aloud. Mrs. Brugha[72] heads poll in Waterford. Incident related by priest at Spiddal—people prevented voting by military. N. Mayo ditto—letter from priest. Protest lodged in Wicklow.—At breakfast P.J. Ryan very excited—startled eyes. I told him that Seán Mulroy *was* in for Co. Cavan. 'But Derry McNeill says he isn't.' But I have seen paper, P.J.,—and he *is*. P.J. accepted with good grace. Describe him.

Showery & wet again. Just before tea a heavy shower began to fall. I had gone out to wash mug plate etc. & was late. As I left the backdoor in rushed 4 men from another hut carrying a sick man on his bed. Rushed out of rain for shelter. Carried away line with shirts sheets etc,—broke & everything falls on muddy ground. Rain pelting hard. Pulled line across door & tried to lift clothes out of dirt. I protested. Threw wet breeches and cap etc. on to my bed. I told them to keep the half of door next my bed, as my bed would be wet. Vexed & cross. Sick man heeding nothing, but lying pale & quiet on pillow. After tea, when I came back, G. Wallace came over to me & said: 'Don't leave any of your parcels, sir, uncovered on your bed. Strangers may come in when the men are out of the hut.' George's respectable manner.

7 p.m. News in per Seán a' Chóta. Got paper from Cookhouse. Up on table & read it out. 'What about the prisoners?' shouted one man in his jocose way. 'That's an idiotic question,' rapped S.K. 'I'm surprised at you' (Nobody heads Sean's vagaries). Election results splendid. Moral victory, considering intimidation, bad register, prisoners in camps etc. Success of 'characters' (Fr. Aiken) and 'gunmen' (Lambert[73], D. Breen etc.) Capt. Redmond in for Waterford—will be a thorn in flesh of Cosgrave. Dr. White 'out'—his Mayoral robes. Shan Lane said: 'He may shut up his shop, sell out & clear from Waterford. We'll hold up our heads when we go back.' Shan Lane's picture framed etc. of Mrs C. Brugha. S. K. drew my attention to it & smiled.—Tried to sleep after tea after dinner. Liam MacDermott with his autograph book. Negatives of photographs of Rath Camp—2 of prisoners in

group killed in this scrap. Copied extract into autograph [book] from *Shears of Destiny* (Atlantic) on Erskine Childers.—Scene in Hut 12 as I entered back door 8.30 p.m. Jubilation re results. Jack Keogh says he'll hold to his original estimate of 53. Brasser, Billy Walsh, J. J. Flanagan, Denis Quille etc. Corkmen running down Cork city & county. –10 p.m. Men marching up & down hut after supper to keep themselves warm—same as in Feb. & March last & in Mountjoy in winter. Fires lighting—smoke—pleasant smell of rashers etc. Card party at lower end of hut—'Deuce, très, ten, knave, honours etc.'

Sat. 1 September 1923

Bright sunny morning. In bed when S. K. came in. Shook his head. 'A fine morning for a turn round the compound before breakfast. Scroungy 12.'—S. K. B Walsh & Gregory Ashe[74] waiting at No. 6 Cookhouse for paper. Long delay. At last H.+ E. [*Ham & Eggs*][75] comes along carrying basket of letters & small parcels. S. K. dodges down side of Hut 6, comes on him outside Hut 12 backdoor. Gets paper slyly. Moved towards Hut 5 followed by others—crowd gathers. Latest returns: 38 Republicans elected. War between Italy and Greece.

As I was shaving myself after inspection young Foley comes in & says: Your friend, the lame man with the crutch is being released.' Went over to Hut 5. Paddy finishing shaving. Surrounded by officers, Lamb, Harte etc. Describe scene. Returned to Hut 12 & finished shaving. Cheers heard. Stapleton in with news of speech. Scene at gate—another speech.

—News that Houlihan is back per Stapleton. Laughter. Men of Hut 5 lined up. Other prisoners who wouldn't sign turned back: but Houlihan taken away again. S. K. says he won't reach Dingle tonight. Letter in from Dingle. Shopkeepers to whom people owed money tell debtors to vote for F. S. Reduced to these tactics. Spoke of P. H's bad temper, 'I couldn't imagine those mild doglike eyes being bad-tempered.' 'But he has the devil of a temper,' said S. K. Enter Staters. 'How's your bulbs. Fine. How's yours?' Slept after tea, but disturbed by Pat Sullivan, in about papers. S. K. in. I knew there was something on his mind.

Went out with him. Told me that he had a reply to those letters sent out on 23 August 1923. Very grateful to S. K. What would life in camp be without letters? Spoke of fixing of bulbs. A winter campaign? But there may be release after the 19th Sept?? Spoke of possible policy of Republican block in regard to abstention or the reverse: war between Italy and Greece may interfere with Cosgrave's plans re Geneva & League of Nations: Greece a misfortunate country. Tino—monkey-like, Venezilos—executions. Turkey's cleverness. Kemal—my namesake.

Over Willie McDermott's bed:

Here's to the rose that buds & blows,
Here's to the ship's in danger
Here's to the lass that turns up her –
To the bould ould Connacht Ranger

Talk in Hut 5 with W MacD & Lynch etc. about the policy of Republicans—abstention or reverse?

– 8 p.m. Dusk gathering in Hut 12. Sleeves of shirts, towels, legs of drawers etc. hanging on lines inside, golden with sunset light thro' western windows. 2 shirts stolen.

Thursday 4 October 1923

Fine cool morning. Frost last night; ground bone-dry. S. K. in. 'Didn't get out letters, after all. Bad luck.' Gave me last night's *Herald* after breakfast. Tim Healy's[76] speech from the throne—full text poor reception. Attendance at Oireachtas by no means exhaustive; Labour keeps away[77]. Fashionably-dressed ladies in gallery—prisoners in rags; the men who won what is gained! Special clause for prisoners. No hope of release. Public safety—*mar eadh* [as if!]. F. S. evidently in a parlous way. Not an Irish idea in it; not the speech of the chief executive of a newly emancipated country with a free parliament. 'Some applause' at end. A frost! a washout! What will John Dillon & Wm. O'Brien[78] think of Tim? Votive Mass in Pro-Cathedral, *coram pontifice* [in the presence of the Pontiff]. The mockery of it. Cosgrave gets a 'somewhat hostile' reception from women & girls. Boohs and hisses. List of nonentities present. Who will think of their names in 20 years time? Miss dear

Desmond's[79] name, but perhaps he is abroad. Tim & Willy both looked on their departure 'in state'. Tim's reputation (such as it is) is *not* growing. 'Tim'd be happier defending some poor bloke in murder case,' said G. Wallace in his slow, West Limerick accent.—News that Ben Sayers of Bray has been released (see 1 October 1923). Only Mulhall & myself from that area remain.—Talk with Billy Walsh and Rocky at end of Hut 13. [']I had a letter from Norah Carroll of Bray (a typist in the Town Hall). She's been released. She's done with men, she says.' 'No wonder,' I commented. 'It makes me ashamed of my sex when I think of how the women in the N.D.U.[80] were treated. Laundry examined by men—you know what women send out. And Irishmen! My God!'

No letters. *Acute* depression. The eternal depression of imprisonment. Depression on a fine day worse than on a wet day. On the latter one can dope oneself with a book—shut the door against it. On a fine day it is different. Memories of depression outside on a warm summer's day. Dust motes; fly buzzing. Shabby blanched look of furniture—the drab look of life. S. K. along after Irish class. 'Jim Stapleton is released. "He knew he'd be released," he said.' Talked with Fr. Stuart. I thought Gogol's *Dead Souls* old-fashioned. But it was published in 1842. No literary form becomes more quickly passé than the novel. 'Dostoevsky', said Frank, 'is as modern in his method as James Joyce.' *War & Peace* is not as old-fashioned as *Anna Karenin* or *Resurrection*. I'm slogging away at W & P. There's a deal of a lot of reading in it. No hope of release. 'We'll be the last to go, I said. 'The young men who carried the guns will be let out: the old young-men with the ideas will be kept in.' Jack Keogh came along as we talked, bundle of papers under his left arm, mufflered, but brisk, in spite of a sad, sad look in his eyes (no wonder).[81] 'I've read in Eire that they assaulted my daughter.' He gave me back the papers that I gave him on Saturday. 'I've read all the Time's Reviews. That article on Lhassa interested me very much.' (He was in India as a 10th Huzzar). 'Might I see them?' asked Frank. 'Papers, I find, are a relief after reading writing, or even reading a book.' I brought him back to Hut 12 & gave him *Times Lity Supplt* & *N. Y. Book Reviews*.—Worked at press-cuttings. Enter James Behan. His character. Teeth:

pipe: shabby, shady look: bachelor: sister. 'You're always working?' 'Yes, I work to keep myself from going mad.' M. Ward along too, looking for information & comment. 'I see.' Very cross & snappy.—Wrote to N. 'Don't be too optimistic. Don't say "Keep up your heart": it loses by repetition.' Dreadful monotony & depression before tea. T. Campbell & Jim Henry practising violin-playing in Hut 12. Protests & laughs by L. Murphy etc. working at rug. 'That's the tune the old cow died of.' 'It's like as if you stood on a dog's tail'—flat notes, etc A tea I noticed signs of madness or queerness in several men. One man (western) rubbing 2 knives together, face up close to them, as if sharpening them. Neiland peering round post in Dining Hall. P. Lawler's face a study—hard, thin set, unshaven, downcast.

– Walked with S. K. after tea. Lovely clear healthy evening. Talked of release. 'I'll be with you as far as Dunleary and help you with your bags. We'll dally on the road. Spend a night in Kildare.' Will avoid 'friends'. 'If Mrs. Stephens offered me tea I'd refuse it. Some would get well-treated when the like of me wouldn't: too proud to stoop. People would say: He's a toff: he doesn't require assistance.' Talked of the beginning of the I. R. A. movement. The meeting in Wynn's Hotel. O'Rahilly's[82] pale face, dark eyes, waxed moustache—sense of humour. His hobbies. S. K. said that Wall came along to him at Irish class & gave him 3 packets of cigarettes which Jim Stapleton sent in from Newbridge. S. K. is reading Lamb's essays. South Sea House. 'You ought to study the characters in the camp—G. Wallace, for instance.' I told him they were all down in my Journal—if I could get it out.—Before lock-up G. Wallace was standing between Huts 12 & 13 watching the sky. 'Fine evening, neighbours!'—the countryman this evening, not the sergeant-major of the Munsters.—H & E locking padlock on backdoor of Hut 5. 'Don't lock it, Ham,' said S. K. 'I'll want to escape tonight.' 'Escape my ballocks!' H & E's clever camouflage—the hard word—the soft heart.—S. K. off. Back with day's paper from H & E. 'I'll let you see it tomorrow.'—9 p.m. Beds out in middle of hut section 4, under electric bulb—men playing cards.

[The following entries relate to the hunger-strike of October and November 1923. The hunger-strike began in Mountjoy, where there was a dispute about 'political' status for IRA prisoners. It spread rapidly to the other jails and camps.

In July 1923 there were over 11,000 military prisoners in the state. There had been a number of releases since then; many, but not all, of those freed had signed a form promising not to bear arms against the government. Campbell's diary (e.g. the entry of 21 August 1923 above) shows how the releases increased the anxiety of those left inside. The discovery, on 12 October 1923 on the Featherbed Mountain near Dublin, of the murdered body of Noel Lemass, Captain of an IRA unit (he had not been seen since his arrest on 3 July) had outraged public opinion and the hunger-strikers may have hoped to benefit by this revulsion.]

Friday 19 October 1923

Night of high wind—but slept well. Did not eat breakfast of Hovis bread and cheese I had set on plate under my bed over night. Meant to breakfast at 5 a.m.—HUNGER-STRIKE begins 6 a.m. for unconditional release.—P. A.'s knocking and running stones along corrugations (they know, as notice of strike was sent to Governor by our O/C before lock-up the previous evening). Enter Six-Co P.A. to Peter White: 'Get your men out of bed by 8 o'c, or they'll be turned out.' Gruff Northern accent. 'He must be a bottle-blower,' said P. Lawler when he was gone. 'Is the rough-stuff going to be used on us?'—Just before Count an officer & P.A. entered and called for Hut Leader. No response. P. White asleep. Went along asking prisoners where the H.L. slept. No response, or very little—'He's along there...' Peter at last found. 'Is there a prisoner of the name of Mick McDonnell in this hut?' Peter said that it was no use asking him, as no numbers or names would be given. 'Very well, will I do it myself?' 'You can do what you like,' said P. W. 'Michael McDonnell!' called out, but no response—nobody of that name in hut. Camouflage to see if names wd. be answered. *Exeunt.*—Jokes and rallying. 'Blow the whistle, Peter. You won't be able to blow it as strong tomorrow.'—S. K. in, very brisk. Eating in Hut 5 until 2 this morning. Pendy & the open shirted fellow from Kilmallock. The salt mackerel sent from Dunquin, the previous evening. 'The Last Supper,' said the open shirted fellow. 'You're like Jesus Christ distributing the loaves and fishes.'—No breakfast, of course. G. Wallace enters from washhouse with towel in hand. Cries of '12 up, George!' 'We've got no bananas today[83].'—Over to cookhouse. Doors locked, padlocked—nothing doing.—Men round stove in Hut 12. Seán Twomey reading aloud from current *Eire* Miss MacSwiney's reply to article in *Irish Statesman* of 22nd September '23. Neiland reading John Mitchel's *Jail Journal*. Rest smoking, talking—rather quietly. The quiet in hut & camp for last few days very noticeable.—Drank water & smoked—but smoking is bad for me.

News in that strike in the Tintowns 1, 2, 3 & Hare Park is in today's paper. Several men removed to hospital from the 'Joy. Batch of prisoners—bandaged—removed from 'Joy to Kilmainham. Crowds outside jail saying rosary & singing hymns. Dev. reported on strike, but rumor not confirmed.—Prisoners being released (11 a.m.) from No 1 Camp. 'Number 1 let you down badly,' said the Cockney to S. K. 'They're answering to their numbers.'—S. K.'s Irish class stopped by order of the Governor. P. A.'s say: 'Nobody allowed in Dining Halls'. S. K.'s legend on the blackboard. Students write it down: (quote) *Táimíd ar stailc oibre (ocrais) ar son ár bhfuascaltha go léir, ar son na poblachta, ar son na h-Éireann. Sé dualgas gach fir in aghaidh gach broide bheith dílis agus, má's gádh é, bás d'fhághail mar fuair Cúchulainn dochlaoidhte.* [We are on hunger-strike to gain release for all of us, for the sake of the Republic, for Ireland. Every man's duty in every emergency is to remain loyal and if necessary to die as did the unconquerable Cúchulainn.]

Talk with Kilroy. 'Men ought to meet and chat.' Kilroy's quiet idealism.—Carpenters removing every fifth board from sheeting in Hut 12. Contract?—Out with S. K. in air. 'My last look at the Wicklow Hills,' said S. K. Clear cold sunny day. Day *very* long. No meals to act as intervals. Joined by old Michael Cronin of Lixnaw. His character, accent and appearance. Cap—red nose—sallow skin,—black gray shave & moustache, brows. 'The priests in Irish movements'—Fenians, Land War, 'they murdered Parnell,' etc. The relatives of prisoners ought to storm the P. P.'s houses. 'Nail up the chapel doors etc.'—Feel myself getting tired & weak. Headache & nausea. Inclined to vomit (sensation as of seasickness). S. K. thinks we'll win by Sunday. I wonder? Prisoners walking in twos & groups—listless, downcast look.—5 p.m. P. Lawler in bed—knees up under blankets—smoking & reading. Jack White (pale & depressed). L. Murphy *very* white & 'jaw-ey'. Headache worse—vacuum & nausea—as I write 4 p.m.—Made bed down. Just as I was about to get in after 'count' enter officer: 'All out for roll-call!' P.W. said no names would be answered. Stood to bed (one stocking off). Names of all prisoners in hut read out by officer in a mechanical way, but no response. Dismiss. Opinion general that the roll-call was so much bluff, just to show that the F. S. was top-dog yet. Tired: slept quickly.

Sat. 20 October 1923

Did not sleep well during night. Heart's action accelerated—blood pounding. Heard the continual gnawing of rats on sheeting, & squeals. Owing to every 5th board being removed they will be in to us, no doubt.—Bunny in during night with Windy Joe—scrutinizing men in bed—Joe's cane, & cap & strut—like a General, no less.—'Count'—most of prisoners in bed. No rough-handling, as expected. J. J. Walsh in with news that 130 men had come in during night from Mtjoy. Got up, shaved & washed. The tonic effect of a shave.—Cookhouses locked—padlocks—groups of prisoners about gates. A big crowd outside 18 Hut where the Mtjoy men are. Also outside Hospital Hut 16.—S. K. asked me had I been over to 18 Hut? 'It's a sight; don't miss it.' Went over. Cakes—currant cakes—in bottom of stony trench opposite door. Make my mouth water. P. A.'s unloading stoves outside—new galvanized pipes—rusty stoves. Prisoners in Camp carrying over bedsteads from Censor's Hut. Went in—picking steps between men stretched on mattresses, wrapt in blankets on floor. Middle of hut cluttered too—sides full—blankets overflowing everywhere. Like a casualty clearing-station after a battle. Men with white, waxen, death-like faces (some lying, some sitting up against wall) & yellowed eyes.

Iodine-stained bandages. Neckcloths round heads with headache. Lips, cracked, dry, blood-caked. Mugs of water. Tintown prisoners setting up beds—hammering, falling of backs & fronts etc. Mick Sheehy—thin but face still with colour—starved look all the same. Enter Bunny & fellow officers, some in civvies. Bunny depressed-looking, gooseberry eyes, rabbit teeth (the archetype of catspaws—men to do the dirty work for pay). Have they hearts or consciences? Over to Hospital 16. J. J. Flanagan very white, appealing eyes: P. Clear, red-bearded, MacGuill of Dundalk, from the 'Joy. One man—Creighton of S. Dublin—very bad. T. P. O'Malley said he didn't expect him to last through the night. Mouth open. Displaced heart. Pushed priest away. 'Tell him to go away. He wants me to take food—I won't.'

The situation in a week's time from today. Opinion rife that F.S. may let 300 men die. They're bankrupt in policy; bankrupt in humanity; bankrupt in civilization.—Wrote letter to N. telling her to hope for best but be prepared for worst. If I die it will be as an agnostic—a believer in the fine heroic things; a disbeliever in the unheroic lies of the Churches.—Men go to confession in large numbers.—Tom Longmore gets letters out by Sentry—borrowed Fruit Salts from me.—Letters in just before lock-up. None for me.—Into bed early. The men from the Joy in 18 Hut have been distributed among other huts—several new men (on hunger strike since Sunday last) in Hut 12. 2 next to G. Wallace near backdoor.

Sunday 21 October 1923

Rats not so busy during the night. Over at cakes in trench opposite 18 Hut? Heard cries of sentries all night: 'No 1 post & all's well' etc—the irony of it. All's wrong in Tintown; in Ireland itself.—Carty down in singlet & bare legs at our stove 5 p.m. [*sic*] Makes it up. Smoked a cigarette—point of red light in darkness. Men restless—springs of beds creaking. Near daylight Peter White got up & sat down in shirt at fire (burning merrily owing to Carty's stoking). 'Are yez all dead, chaps?—in adenoidal Dublin accent. 'Surely some of yez is alive!' Weak on rising, but got up. S. K. in, very—almost forcedly—brisk. S. K.'s little kink of vanity.—Great many of men in 12 Hut in bed. Lots in 5 Hut too.—Walk round in air. We live on air now—air & water—2 elemental life giving things. Better to die in our boots like soldiers, if we *are* to die.—Seán Kavanagh brought in *Sunday Independent*. Little publicity given to hunger-strike. Conspiracy of silence. 'Change of Abode' (in reference to transfer from 'Joy)—'Prisoners refuse food' the captions. How different in the Tan days. But it was British then; now it's West British are the enemy. Incident at Mullingar Cathedral. Rosary said in church by layman: Adm[inistrator]'s protest.—Few prisoners returning from Mass in 18 Hut say the priest gave no sermon—said nothing—not a word of comfort to men anhungered for an ideal. Callousness, materialism of clergy.—Men very quiet all day—talk in low tones around stove. Mugs on stoves—salt & water—pepper—'soup'. Like old women, mollycoddles. Men from the 'Joy stand it well after 7 days of it. Young fellow with smiling teeth & budding moustache from Golden Ball[84]. 'Do you know me?' I didn't know him. Remembered me from early volunteering days. He knew my voice, he said, as he heard me reading up the hut. His opinion of Glencullen & the Ball. Begley not out. His car taken & returned by O'Rourke. Enniskerry, bad as it is, is better.—Brought paper over to Billy Walsh in 13 Hut—in bed—face flushed (bad heart) but cheerful.—News in that Brown a Belfastman is taking food—went over with mug and plate to P. A.'s. Has not come back. Hopes that the strike will not be broken—Talk of destruction of food: it's a sin to destroy good food. The bonfire at end of washhouse on Friday morning. My Hovis loaves etc. A. P.A. seen sticking his teeth & fingernails into a Michaelmas goose (roast) for one of the prisoners—in Parcel Office. 'Devoured it like a dog.'—S. K. is excited. Beef coming into camp! Two big pots—strangers—in with Billy Byrne.—Went over to cookhouse 6 and saw sides of beef being unloaded from a military horse-wagon. 2 officers—one in light grey raincoat—doctors? C. Byrne & B. Byrne in close conversation—smiling too. Is it good news? Seán Kennedy outside Hut 5 (crowd clustered there) has a story that 'all prisoners will be released by a certain date if men renege hunger-strike.' But C. Byrne contradicts it to excited group of prisoners which gathers round. B. Byrne, he says, says that his Govt. take up a strong attitude. I told him: 'So do we.' General fall of spirits. *I* am very low. S. K. serious and pale.—Over to Hospital 16. T. P. O'Malley, Dr. Comer, Paddy McDonnell, Fr. Daly etc. in dispensary. T.P. serious. Doctors say that they will not give medical attendance to any man on hunger strike. No man hunger-striking will be removed to Curragh Hosp. Does it mean that they will let us die? F.S. capable of anything.—Over to Hut 6 with S. K. Gave me legend from Irish class written on blackboard (see Friday 19th Oct). Walked up & down deserted hut—cold outside. S. K. optimistic suddenly. 'We'll get through.' Billy Byrne's smile—? Captain Murphy's story:—'the troops must eat in the morning.' 'Does it mean that we will be forced to eat?' 'Oh no, there'll be nothing of that.' In cheerfuller mood (it's all mental) but the news is too good, I feel, to be true. S. K. takes letter. Volunteer F– n, address etc. etc. (I wrote it down). *May* get out MS. tomorrow night.—S. K. into Hut 12 before lock-up. 'They're out in the compound in camp 3, with bags etc.—a search? rough-stuff.' 'Bread has come in!' 'Is it soup & bread in the huts tomorrow?'—Lock-up. Made down bed. Men round stove talking of royal feeds (like the bard in the vision of MacConglinne[85])—beefsteak & lobster salad—too strong—'what about scones oozing with butter, & tea?' 'beef-tea from the cookhouse would satisfy me.'—sweet cake—Hovis bread & marmalade—poached eggs—'nicely browned Cambridge sausages & rashers'—'Ah, cold apple-cake would be nice!' 'Ah,' said Paddy Lawler from his bed, (smoking, knees up under blanket) 'I'd eat a child's arse through a chair this minute.' Into bed. Flake meal and sugar.—Fell asleep, not depressed, almost cheerful.

Mon 22 October 1923

I had a smoke of the pipe in the darkness of the hut before reveillé. Reveillé—bugle in wind—but we are not fit to rise, all nigher to death than ever before—Stove made up by Benny Shiels (in shirt & bare legs)—joking—with the hearty little laugh peculiar to him—as usual. Knocking at door: not so insistent as usual—the P.A. knows. Nobody up for Count. Something doing today? Soup left in in buckets to tempt us? I hear that the men were put out in compound of Camp 3 yesterday afternoon to enable P. A.'s to put grub in huts—no success, however.—I get up. Bring mug of fresh water to G. Wallace in bed. (The 'cup of cold water' of Gospels—will I get credit for it?) Out to washhouse to wash teeth etc.—nothing to be seen but a latrine bucket outside Hut 10. Fresh, cold morning, but dry. Compound deserted. I shave. Jack Staunton says: 'Don't—the new growth will take it out of you'. All the men in bed. Hut unswept; only latrine buckets emptied.—S. K. in. Yesterday's meat, he says, was removed & a fresh supply in. Contract? or deliberate policy? Nothing doing—no soup or bread, as expected—but it seems the P. A.'s knocked up cooks this morning as usual.—Over to Hut 5. Groups round stove; majority in bed. Feel no worse than yesterday. Whistle goes for inspection. S. K. handed day's *Independent* by Billy Walsh's friend in civvies.—Back to Hut 12 and sat round stove. One is restless and inclined not to settle long at anything. Men very quiet—2 Mountjoy men, G. Wallace's cousins—in bed at back door. We talk of death (a good deal of death)—a little of victory. Like men trapped in a mine, or in an open boat at sea. G Wallace's worn, red, pimply, unshaven face (reddish beard, which never looks well growing).—S. K. brings paper. I read it aloud to group. 'It took a lot out of me,' said S. K. 'reading it in 5.' F. S. meeting in College Green—10,000 present—usual procession headed by Mrs. Despard and Mme. MacBride pushed back by D.M.P. Boosting of Kennedy K.C.[86] Die-hard attitude (low-type speeches) of Cosgrave & Blythe[87]—no release for prisoners.—Republican rally same venue in evening—large attendance. O'Mullane speaks of Noel Lemass's ghost in S. Dublin. Inquest on today. Reference to prisoners on hunger strike (I am short of wind as I read—heat of stove weakening). Seán MacBride escapes from ambulance on transfer from 'Joy to Kilmainham. Rescue? Version obviously a lying one. But truth is not in Irish papers. Rosary and processions all over country, Jim Larkin speaks at meeting in O'Connell street. Talks of general strike—getting machinery ready for end of week. Clare Republicans & Labour men confer in Ennis—ready to down tools. Depressed, silent group from upper end of hut gather round to listen as I read. S. K. brings paper over to Billy Walsh in bed in 13 Hut.—Inspection—informal—Bunny & Kennedy (ex-Tan) pass down hut—K. with cane and gloves. Sneering (yet depressed fed-up) look. Prisoners say nothing. K. gives great look at Calendar over my bed as he passes.—Meet S. K. Over with him to Hut 1 to tell Fr. Stuart about S. MacBride's escape. Impression of hut. Fr. Stuart (face more haggard, & unshaven down) & H. Johnston (beard, red, fully grown) in bed—all hut, too, with exception of 3 or 4 round stoves. Smell of death. What will the huts be like in a week's time—unswept—papers, cigarette packets—latrine buckets flowing over—shambles? Very cold wind sweeping over compound from N. W. Gulls circling in ones & twos. Crows cawing. Rumour in by S. K. about 5.30 p.m. that the Governor had been called to Dublin. What does it mean? Rumour also that Austin Stack[88] has been released from 'Joy.—Made down bed. Wrote letter to Governor asking him to inform my wife if my medical adviser might be permitted to see me. Wrote also to N. (enclosed in Governor's envelope) telling her to send Dr. Taylor of Bray in to me.—Into bed. Everything quiet in hut. G. Wallace (back view—cap pulled over back of neck, hunched shoulders in brown coat greasy from cookhouse) & about 6 others sitting round stove talking very quietly. The conversation turns on bakehouses & their products. Peter White's voice—an exponent—worked in Bolands—never anywhere long. The old journeyman baker. 'What do you know about it—you're only a boy.' The 'Ledgers' in Thompson's Cork—weekend job men. The ordinary life of the hut non-existent. 'J. J.' in bed. No shouting, no songs, no flute, no fiddle, no roughhouse—ceased entirely. Heart easier than previous night.

Tuesday 23 October 1923

Heavy rain all night. Slept little.—S.K. came to me in washhouse with news. If he doesn't find me in one place, he will in another. Phil Cosgrave[89] dead. I talked (loudly) about Mtjoy & execution of Rory O'Connor etc. 'I hope he'll get more justice in the next world than he gave us in the 'Joy.—Couldn't have better luck. Well Sunday, dead Monday.' A workman in bowler hat is hammering a nail with a stone—hammer mislaid. (Futility of job—putting in time.) Revolvered P.A. sitting on wash-bench, kicking his legs (he listens as I talk). C.I.D. to be disbanded—'owing to return to normal conditions'. Is it good news for us? History of C.I.D.—Back to 12 Hut. Told P. J. R –[*Ryan*] (adjutant) lying in bed reading. He opened his old foxy eyes wide & let out a whistle. 'The C.I.D. disbanded? Stick it lads, stick it!' (in hoarse voice to rows of beds). Got into bed again (for propaganda sake). Reading *Freeman*. Governor comes along with other officers. 'Is your name Campbell?' 'Yes.' 'You wrote that letter?' 'Yes.' 'I've sent your request along to H.Q. I'll let you know later.' Civil—decent little man. Bunny came in ½ hour later. 'A letter for ye from Governor.' Handed me letter enclosed in envelope addressed to N. with letter to her enclosed. As I read several men are sitting round stove 4 gloomily brooding heads in hands etc. Majority in bed. 'Better to stay in bed—there's too many up. They'll use it as Propaganda. The priest is talking about it. "It's a farce," he said. "See the men in the compound etc."'—3 p.m. Whistle blown in Hut by P. White. Order countermanded. New order from H.Q. 'Men to answer names & numbers.' MacMahon (Ennis), Jackie Farrell (face burnt by petrol) released. Handshaking. 'Tell them about the strike outside.'—Buckshee doctor in uniform with Socko as orderly. Surgeon probationer. 3rd medical. Puts hands over bad men's hearts—no stethoscope.—5 p.m. Young Fitzgerald (Mtjoy) bad. Gasping. Can't make water. Priest sent for urgently—Count 6 p.m. Prisoners in bed: those up loll on beds. Nobody 'standing to'.—9 p.m., as I am in bed awake, backdoor opens & enter priest & I.O.[90] Lamb. Cold damp air from outside—door left open. Priest comes after being sent for 4 hours ago. Half callous, half apologetic. 'There's only 3 of us for 3 camps of 3200 men.' Goes up to Fitzgerald's bed. Lamb's fat, wellfed figure standing silhouetted against electric light. Priest comes down hut & goes to Mtjoy man opposite my bed. Keeps hat on all the time. Smug, unspiritual look. Talks with P. White. Group round stove 4—L. Murphy drawn white face listening. 'What'd he say, Peter?' 'He says no man will get ministration unless he goes off hunger-strike.' Paddy Sullivan rates against priests (Paddy is a pious Catholic, most devoted to practices of religion). His Cork voice is highpitched, weak, hoarse, querulous. (Voice changed a lot owing to hunger). P.J. R—along. He stops as he passes my bed. 'Everything's going all right, Joseph. We've only to endure.'

Wed. 24 October 1923

Seán Kavanagh in with news of jury's finding in Noel Lemass case. Verdict of murder. Govt. forces implicated in murder *and* removal of body to Featherbed. Inquiry suggested. 'If I were N. Lemass's father, I'd insist on a commission. Public security is at stake. There's a precedent in the Sheehy-Skeffington[91] case. Decency of British. Sent over one of their biggest lawyers, Sir J. Simon.' Two baskets of letters & small parcels in. 3 letters for me from N. dated 18th 21st and 23rd Oct. (quote). Bill from Land Bank. Drat! why don't people outside have *savoir faire?*—Got (imaginary) weak fit, but got up. 'I'll die in my boots if I'm to die at all,' I thought. Went out. Walked with S. K. in brisk wind. Fresher & stronger. 'We'll keep game to the last,' said S.K. with bravado (and spirit, too). Round the compound once. Nobody about. Imaginarily tired. Windblown late Autumn clouds. Cruachan Kinsella & hills grey, misty-blue—appearing & disappearing. People & motors going to Curragh races. The racing crowd—much *they* care for idealism or for human suffering. The Hedonistic Philosophy: the Stoic ditto.—Into Hut 5. Kilroy, yellow white, dark beard talks of the defections from strike in Camp. He excused them. 'After all, think of the 12 apostles. Even Peter ran away. We're only poor human beings. We're not so bad at all.' His real simple religious sincerity. S.K. twitted him on his unshaven appearance. 'I'll go out this way. I'll let the Mayo people see what they did on me!' S.K said he thought it was better to shave & keep clean.—Over to Fr. Stuart in Hut 1. Fr. in bed. His wife was down yesterday. Doherty brought in a message, with hot-water bag & parcel of lemons. D. very civil. Frank's estimate of him. 'He's one of the worst of them—because he's so smug outwardly. An Ardee man.

The Dundalk men know him.' Lent me *Irish Statesman* of 13th Oct. (quote).—8 p.m. From the Stove (4) red cinders fall out on floor. I count them—seven. 'It will last seven days,' I said oracularly. 'It will be over by Saturday. I'm superstitious, you know. Messages often come to me in that way etc.' G. Wallace talking: the philosopher always. 'We'll win, Mr. Campbell—we *will*!' He spoke of the racing crowd disparagingly. 'A full belly & pleasure is all they care about.'

Thursday 25 October 1923

Third anniversary of death of Terence MacSwiney by hunger-strike. (Reminiscences of 'funeral'[92] in Dublin; Gogarty's death-mask HUNGER). Polling in S. Dublin City election.—Slept on & off during night.—S. K. in. 'Good morning, Chieftain!' I heard him say (I was in a doze, my head averted). 'He's asleep, I think,' said J. J. Walsh. S. K. went off. Got up. Gave gargle of salt & water to Ned Enright (Mtjoy man)—sore throat, no wonder after his experiences of hardship. Made up stove. All men in bed except Carty & B. Brady of Cavan—a hard man. Hut deadly still. Unswept. Latrine buckets unemptied; stink owing to no Bacilikil. Ashes accumulated round Stove 4, papers, pieces of firewood, cigarette packets littering floor. No medical attendance of any kind, or visit from Governor or staff, or P. A. itself.—Kerry prisoner in (reddish hair & clipped moustache, an ex-soldier) says two men—Moran of Tipp. (angashore of labourer's son) & Peadar Ó Máille of Spiddal were removed on stretchers from Hospital 16 last night. Two men also out of No 1 Hut & 1 out of No 4 Hut. Creighton still lingering on—marvellous hold of life. Young Fitzgerald (Hut 12) ditto. Heard heavy clatter of men coming from Mass in 18 Hut—mostly communicants. About 200, I hear, attended out of 1400 odd.—Out to washhouse. Cold wind from N. W. Sunny, but rain fell during the early morning & the ground is wet & puddly. I see two P. A.'s carrying out a bed with a weak man in it, swathed up in blankets.—Noticed papers stuck on door of Hospital 16. Went over & copied them. 'No salts or opening medicine. You will be notified when there is a further supply. T.P. OM.' '*Please Notice*: That the patients in this hut are *very weak*, & do not wish to see *any visitors*. Do not knock at the door.'—Weak somewhat—first time I felt it. This is the 7th day.—Over to Hut 5. Sat round stove talking to Sean Quilter (describe his appearance—weak—pinched—hunched—but full of gameness of spirit). Landers (hair on end, like a clown's, red face, strong & defiant) etc. 'We'll beat them if we stand firm. It's a test of the morale of the I. R. A.' I spoke of the *Trevessa*. 'If 300 deaths take place will F. Aiken countermand the order. General attacks position—fails—casualties—retreats. A big blow for us, no doubt.'—S.K. in. 'I'm promised the paper.' Difficult to get owing to Governor's blockade. No propaganda apparently, favourable to prisoners to get through. S. K. very fidgety. Cannot sit down. Hands in pockets, set face—in & out all the time scenting out news. At last he brings it in—a new unused paper—*had* to pay for it. 'These fellows haven't a red!' Had to move back from fire. Heat weakens me, cold strengthens me. (Blake's proverb.) S. K. reads news. Half column given to hunger-strike on second page. Conspiracy of silence. Shame on Ireland! S. F. organisation appeals to Bishops. Tintown 3 incident of Sunday—men out in rain for 1 1/2 hours. Hot water supply cut off, men have to wreck the huts owing to no firewood etc.

Names of men in Kilmainham given—E. O' Malley (weak), Stack, G. Plunkett, M. Kilroy, Fr. Gallagher, David Robinson[93] etc. No Labour action—the dockers of Dublin have gone back. Rottenness of Irish Labour. Processions hosed in Tipperary & Dundalk. Two raids on Civic Guards barracks—sergeant shot in Tournafulla, Co. Limerick. Camouflage to draw attention off prisoners & show disturbed state of country? Kennedy not too confident in S. Dublin city. Display advt—Big Hunger Strike Demonstration in O'Connell St, Dublin tonight 8 p.m. Opinion that nothing will be done until after the election.—Told S.K. I meant to break up MS. & distribute through clothes. Tomorrow or next day I may be too weak to do it.—Back to Hut 12. Weak; but bring in can of water & distribute it to men in 4 section. All eager to hear news. Faces over blankets. Deadly quiet—not a sound. Wind soughing wintrily outside. Carried out stinking latrine bucket & dashed water into it in washhouse.—Back to Hut 12 & into bed. Must conserve my strength. Wrote these notes.—C. Byrne in; mottled red face, ignorant air, bald reddish head. 'These fellows will put you to the very extreme test.' 3 weeks. 'If Mary Mac stuck it, surely *we* can.'[94] In a day or two there will be no water, no fires etc. Press against us—publicity is everything in a hunger-strike, otherwise we die like rats in a hole. Priest in to say Mass says that the Hunger-strike is a fraud. 'He's a callous whore.'—No letters. A few parcels in—'mostly empty boxes' says an orderly as he passes carrying one end of a blanket—nothing for me. No sorting or censoring is done on a Curragh race day. Racing goes on in spite of suffering.—2 p.m. Joe Cullen, Arigna, says they are putting stoves in Hut 7. What for? Medical orderlies? P. A.s?—P. White gets up & staggers around stove with boots unlaced. Glandular, spits. Tries to sing—but cannot.—So restless, I cannot read, or settle to anything.—Prisoner with Limerick accent in from Hut 3. Two men bad there. 'Dep. Gov. Prendergast says he can't recommend them for release—he'd have to recommend the whole camp. It won't last more than 2 days. I know what hunger-striking is; I'd experience of it myself.' Colossal undertaking for Govt. if all men collapse. This prisoner tells me he was on hunger-strike in Cork during Tan War; shifted to Wormwood Scrubbs; broke it on boat, crossing, on doctor's orders; resumed later for 14 days in Scrubbs. No ill effect afterwards. Old Michael Cronin sticking it wonderfully. 'Old men stand hardship better than young men.'—*HUNGER—Describe sensations.*—3 p.m. Director of Medical Services for Curragh Command (Dr. Madden) comes into Camp. Is the wind up? Something in the way of medical attention may be given. It is about time.

12 midnight. 3 P. A.'s come into Hut 12. They leave back door open. One of them addresses another as Sergeant. Is it the F. S. Q.M.? He goes over to Shinners' bed—talks with P. Lawler. 'Why don't you let the fellow out & he'll take medicine & food?' Talk of prisoners in bed after they go out. 'A buckshee doctor! It is the Q.M.—I know his phiz,' said L. Murphy. Relapse into silence.

Fri. 26 October 1923

Absolute quiet & deadness in the Hut. Rows of beds on either side—grey blankets—sheets (in various stages of dirt & greyness) *à la* lifeboat—men strong, weak, shaved, unshaved, some asleep, some reading, some brooding into the ceiling of the hut, some smoking pipes, some fags. Hut filthy—dust, ashes, papers, sputum everywhere.—Got up—made bed in military fashion—washed in wash-house. Nobody about; a city of the dead. Fine, but cold. Doherty (pale, fat, furtive) gives me a look as he passes—I am the only one about.—B-r-r-r-r—grating of gears—I looked out & saw the grey Red Cross ambulance drive up past Black House & towards Hospital 16. (The hospital that is not a hospital). Creighton removed.—Back to Hut 12. Men in bed ask me 'what's the news?' as I enter towel etc in hand. A man asks me to get him a light from Carty's stove (going since early morning—Carty was up in the dark driving the end of the sweeping brush into it to clear it of ashes). The hut looks dirtier than when I went out.—S. K. *not* in. What's up? An unusual thing for him not to appear, grave or smiling, with news or without it.—Made press-cuttings in preparation for removal alive or dead. S. K. along as I work. Bad news. Depressed, pale, wind short. Government statement in framed square, heavy letters. No releases of prisoners on hunger-strike. Usual releases—all—stopped. Canvassed opinion. Bluff? Sean Twomey (from his bed—toothless) thinks it is *not* bluff. I, personally, think it is 'face-saving': another policy, unshown, up their sleeve. Something must happen—Over to Hut 5 & sat at No 2 stove. Men weary & depressed.—Over to Hut 1 to see Fr. Stuart. Talked with Fr. Garland, sitting at stove—face rubicund & unchanged, eyes as brown & cheery as ever (fascinating face). 'I can stick it for two months,' he said. 'But *can* he?' asked S.K. 'The old engine can't work if it is not stoked.' Over to Fr. Stuart's bed. Fr's eyes clear—his shy, frank look—face thin & sunken with young man's down on chin. *Nation & Atheneum* (current) lying on floor. Picked it up & read it. Reference in political notes (Irish correspondent) to Noel Lemass's murder & hunger-strike on big scale (quote).—Out again in keen wind. The wind makes me strong—tonic to blood & heart. Paddy Landers (tangle of hair blowing): 'Jesus Christ, it's a mad policy. It will fail. A pack of bloody idiots in the 'Joy started it. Frank Aiken's full belly. I've my living to earn. As soon as I feel weak I'll walk out of the gate & get grub. The foolishness of dying for Ireland to put a pack of lousers in power. No Robert Emmet for me!' I caught the depression. F. S. Officers pass along—Galvin; Barnett (hands in pocket, red nose) no gentlemen. Callous, *worried* look on faces. Cook-house chimneys going. More men are giving in their guns—going for food. Their beds are removed to hut 7 where they eat and sleep, apart from others. Met T.P. O'Malley coming from latrine (hairy open chest). He is optimistic. 'We're winning!' (I doubted him). He tells me that only 40,000 recorded votes in S. Dublin city election out of 78,000. 46,000 in last election. Big gain to Republican vote; F.S. supporters apathetic. In with him into hospital. Gave me salts. Old C. Byrne writing at table at top. Talked with McGuill (Dundalk—cheery), J.J. Flanagan (very worn, bright, appealing eyes), Fr. Daly, P. Clear (Paddy not the 'next best thing'). Enquiries for news, morning paper. J. J. Flanagan suggests Publicity Bureau & propaganda round camp. 'That's for the Camp Council,' I said. 'They resent advice'. Silence in Hut 12. Ambulance heard going all the day; effect on one's nerves like that of the rattling tumbrils on the scared people of Paris in 1789. At stove 4 L. Murphy & P. Sullivan (pinched waxen nose) very depressed. 'It's inhuman. Hunger-strike last weapon—never again.' I talked of Fort George & the conditions there after '98—Leigh Hunt, Bunyan, Walter Raleigh. Murphy knew Raleigh's cottage at Youghal.—Tom Rynne comes in back door carrying heavy mail bag over shoulders—letters. One from N. (dated 24th Oct—quote). Cheered. Weakish—but it is largely a mental attitude. Able to walk & carry water. *Not* hungry. S. K. in: very secretive. 'I've a new line—Barnett'. I don't trust that fellow. 'Don't be downhearted,' says Seán. Over to hospital with him. Raining. Read N.'s letter re going to Mme. O Rahilly's.[95] 'I did her many a good turn in Kerry'. Slightly changed attitude of F. S. doctors. '*Won't* you take medicine, food etc'—an appeal rather than a threat or indifference.—Coal fatigues going out in spite of yesterday's order to the contrary. F. S.Q.M. says special fatigues—the rotters—will be on tomorrow. Over to Hut 5. S. K. in critical mood—'4 camp administrators—*all* bad—couldn't run a shit-house'.—Lock-up 6 p.m. Broke up packet of MS. & distributed among clothes. G. Wallace sits on my bed & talks. 'Anything new? What does S. a chóta think now? Has he had a wire? He seems more cheerful than in the morning.'—Round stove 4 Maryboro' men are talking of Christmas in prison. Another Christmas? Last Christmas—turkeys—whiskey, port wine etc. Gave specially made-up parcels to poor men—men from 6 counties—'with compts. of fellow-prisoners'. Hallow Eve on 31st—apples, nuts—will we be out for them? 'I would eat an apple—it wd. bring me back from the grave,' said Neiland pathetically. 'The *very opposite*, at the present moment,' I said. Restaurants—mixed grill at Dolphin, Red Bank, Bonne Bouche, the Dive (its proprietor an ex D. M. P. man), the Bailey, little fish & chip saloon in Crampton Court, 'very clean' said Jack White. Talk of madmen of Camp: Siki—Fitzsimons (dangerous), the fellow in Hut 13—Felim Malone.

Sat. 27 October 1923

Heavy rain all night. S. K. in about 10.30 a.m.—I was still in bed. Whispered (bending over me) ' I may be able to get that out tonight'. News of O'Mullane's[96] defeat in S. City Dublin by large majority. Got up. Went out to wash-house & washed. Talked with Shanahan who came in. Pale & pinched peasant type from Kerry. 'I've a mother at home to support—little brothers & sisters—I'm going out to eat.' First break in Hut 12. Didn't blame the poor beggar. Hunger is a terrible tempter. Rain! Rain! Rain! Nobody about. A city of the dead. Ambulance not out today—all bad cases removed. C. Byrne came in to P. J. R.'s bed with day's paper. Went up, sat down on bed-edge & listened to him as he read haltingly, with various confections like: 'What else could you expect?' 'The whore's bastard!'. 'The louser!' etc. Kennedy's majority some 12,000 odd. Republican poll 11,000—increase of 2000 on Gen. election figures. About 30000 electors did not vote. The effective vote in constituency was about 60,000. Little publicity given to hunger-strike—but that on *front* page. Procession hosed in Sligo (male members). Various bodies pass resolutions re release; others reject it (the Macroom resolution). He finished reading. 'We're beaten', I said. 'Beaten!' exclaimed P.J. R. C. B. resented what I said that 'the men of intelligence saw the breakaway in the camp'. 'The men of intelligence ought to go out and eat then.' I spoke of S.K. 'Who'd heed Seán K.?' said C. B. Left in dudgeon.—Telegrams (green envelopes) arrive for prisoners. Anxiety of relatives outside. Talk with Seán. Told him about interview with C. B. 'What did he say?' etc. Over to Hut 5. Men in bed & around stoves, depressed. Lee of Waldorf Astoria N. Y. Gold tooth, unshaven. His home in Kerry. When I left N. Y. a friend said 'You're going, & you'll be arrested in a couple of months.' 'God-darned country—no living for an honest man here'. Showed me photographs of Kerry home (small hotel) wife, 'kiddies'—wedding-group in N. Y. in Kilts & Celtic costume, pageant, outing in Central Park N. Y. etc—Irish life of N. Y.—Sense of general stampede. Shinners' bed carried out—Shinners' face flushed, eyes shut. Wire from home—his mother has a heart attack. J.J. Walsh gone—'sneaked out'. Barnett & P. A.'s come in for bed & belongings. Go out with it. Huts 6 & 7 full. Eggs & milk for men off strike. Met Pendy in latrine. His two-facedness. One of the strike-breakers—one of the two who broke into Cookhouse & stole loaves. And yet he pretended to me to be still on strike. Tralee back-laner. Circus-follower. Soldier. The avalanche dates from that incident.—Lots of men go to confession. Biscuit says he'll go 'in God's name'. 'I'll die a good Gaelic pagan, if I'm to die at all'. About 4 p.m. rumour that 46 had gone out of Hut 4. 6 already out of Hut 12—including young Duffy of Kilmovee who walked out carrying bed, manfully & bravely before all the men. Roughly, 300 stampeded out of whole camp. 5 p.m. General clearance. Huts 5 & 4 cleared by Staters. The scene—Deputy officers, P. A.'s, prisoners being hustled into other huts. S. K. pale and excited tells me he's going to Hut 9, beside Old Man Keogh. S. K. says 'It's an upset. This will prevent me seeing H + E [*Ham & Eggs*] tonight'. C. Byrne in middle of group, S. Goodfellow, Johnston etc. in Mud Avenue. 'Call it off, Christy. It's the only thing for it,' I said. He moves away to Hut 12. 'The Camp Council will meet tomorrow & decide.'—The scene in Hut 12. Seán Keogh in, face beard & dirty after 6 days in bed—first two with 'excruciating pains in kidneys.' '12 is the only Hut I see is pessimistic in this Camp,' he said. 'We've reason to be pessimistic,' I replied. 'We're beaten. Bad leadership has beaten us.' Need of publicity bureau, someone to cheer prisoners etc. Back door open—damp air outside & wet under foot. Ned Enright's bed (sick, bearded, dirty, 14 days on strike, from the Joy) pulled back into middle of floor. Fierce draught. Other beds dragged in by P. A.'s—green uniform, shining brass buttons. Raining now. Groups of hunched, cowering men (like seamen, curiously) round little stove 4, burning brightly. They turn round, individually, to see the bed dragged in. Liam Murphy, face lathered, shaving, is pushed unceremoniously aside by Kennedy, shoving in an extra bed from another hut. Strange faces everywhere—big tall fellows in trench coats & scarves come & go with bags etc. (Kitbags, flour-bags, trunks, paper parcels etc.) The strike is visibly & tangibly broken.—No count: not worth while. As I write this I'm feeling sick & groggy—sick at heart. Men removed from Hut 5 (familiar faces, don't know names) come up to me & discuss situation. 'We can't stick it. Flesh and blood can't stand it. A hunger-strike is different to any other order. It'll mean the break-up of the whole organisation. When we're let down, what can we do'? etc etc. One man makes up his mind suddenly. 'I'll take food. I'll go back to No 5 now'. Opens door into rainy darkness & goes out silently. Beds & prisoners' heavy boots going in a stream outside.—No rosary.—Group of wiseacres round stove, the Cork group, as usual, to the fore. 'It's all up, George,' I said to George Wallace, with the knowledge that comes of certainty. 'I'm fed up. I'll sign the form & go out. It's a terrible confession to make after 15 months in jail & 20 years in the movement'. To bed, sick, hungry, weak, depressed, hopeless.

Sunday 28 October 1923

Fine, cold morning. Liam Murphy, P. Sullivan, G. Wallace etc. go to communion.—Great stampede of food-takers during the night. It began after lock-up. Heavy tread of men & P. A.'s passing to Huts 4 & 5 with beds etc. It continues this morning. The men don't care if they are seen now, so many are going. Big number of Tommies in to reinforce P. A.'s. Small physique—merino belts & guns. They are not hostile—in fact, friendly. When I came in after washing & shaving a piece of paper was on my bed. Threw it on floor. 'That's your ballot-paper, sir,' said Corky Ryan, section leader No 4. 'How'll you vote?' I heard somebody asking S. Gormley (in bed). 'A Big No!' I voted a Big No, too.—Out into Fifth Avenue. Met Foley Vice Commdt & Jerry Myles. Foley looked thin, starved & dog-gone—much the same look as Martin O'Regan & Buttimer had after the debâcle of the 24th of April[97] last. How some men wilt under trouble—physical look changed. Jerry Myles[98] devil-may-care attitude—the gunman type. 'What's going to happen now?' I asked. 'Oh, we'll beat them,' said Foley sadly. I had my doubts. The 'official' mind—like a ship's officer telling a windy passenger all was well, when the truth was that all was *not* well.—Sat round stove Hut 12. S. Twomey. B. Brady (cam), L. Murphy etc. I talked of bees—Parthenogenesis etc. etc. Men greatly interested. Anyone talking of what he *knows* is always interesting. S—Twomey & the straw-skeps of the farms of W. Cork as a child.—Votes counted. Only 253 for continuing strike. No official announcement, but figures circulated by word of mouth. S. K. told me he didn't vote. Neither did S. Keogh (with whom he has been talking—beds in No 9 Hut beside each other). 'I wasn't asked for my opinion before the strike was called; I'm not going to give it now after 10 days. It's simply a dodge to get the Camp Council out of trouble.' Considerable relief, all the same.—About 4.30 p.m. a big rush towards gate. Everybody going, carrying a mug (some trying to conceal it, others going with bravado.) 'The strike is called off' 'But is it?—I'll wait for the official announcement'—but all the same the speaker went too. I went. Scene outside P. A.'s Hut immediately beyond wire gate. Big strong men without a feather out of them—colour, spirits the same. Others—P. Hogan etc—looking pale, starved & miserable. The struggle for food—N. York Bread Line—soup kitchen. M. Rooney, Seán Farrell, Sean Robinson etc. Talk &

comments—but mostly silent. Old Mick Cronin—nose blue in cold—standing aside with his mug. 'Let the old man in,' I appealed. He was pushed into the door of the already full Hut. Inside 2 P. A.'s (big Newell & another Northern man) were dispensing milk & eggs. A soup bucket is handed out. 'Hot water.' 'Siki—fill that with milk.' 'Egan, more eggs' (box of eggs in straw pushed through press of men). I got in after long waiting. My name, number, hut etc. taken by Northern. 'That's all right, *Joe*' (very friendly). Newell asked me would I take a duck egg—he had a big, green-shelled egg in his hand. 'No, I'd rather have a hen-egg. A duck's too strong.' He broke it into the [½] mug of milk. In a whisper (the stock of his gun—with criss-cross engraving—sticking out of holster):—'Is Seán Kavanagh coming out?' I told him that he likely would.—I went to the door of hut. 'Well, here's luck—we'll be friends one day, I hope. 'I hope we will,' said the Northern P. A. 'Oh, that's good' as I gulped the flip down, handing my fork to P. Hogan 'after 10 days' starvation. The damned country is not worth all this suffering.' 'It's *not,*' said the P.A. Exit to make room for others.—At the Cookhouse 7 the F. S. Q. M. was working hard (pale-faced, cap stuck on back of head)—tea etc. being handed out to men already off strike. 'Damn your soul stand back!' 'Jasus Christ, have a heart' etc.—As I passed down Mud Avenue with mug, Mick Staunton gave an unfriendly glare at me.—Order given for men moved temporarily into strange huts to return to their own. Beds being carried back. All bustle & noise & laughing & chaffing. The reaction to strain & silence. Outside Hut 6 a friendly red-haired P. A. said to me: 'We're carrying out what we carried in this morning.' 'That's the way of the world,' I replied. Mick Rooney with brush in hand tidies up filth of Hut 12—other men sweeping. 'The weight of the dirt is gone—the hut'll look a lot cleaner.' Mick's character. [S. Twomey in washhouse: 'As soon as I can get off it with honour I will' 'I will not go off it' (*illegible*)]—Round stove in evening after lock-up. P. Hogan's relief. 'I'm feeling powerful. Ach, it's inhuman—it's the last weapon to be used.' No music, but a lot of life & conversation. Men in bed for 10 days are up & about. Benny MacNally: 'I'm feeling great after that drop o' milk.' Jack White & others got none—still pale & depressed. The talkers are not the heroes—they talk, however after the battle as if they had done everything.—Back-door opens about 10 p.m. 'Get the men to stand to their beds.' (Joe greasy & black face, arms tucked up). Buckets of soup & bread are brought in & given out. Tea later. Lights left on—P. A.'s not over officious or apparent. Relief—then disappointment. 'What will the other Camps say of us?' Bad leadership the cause—the men are all right—just an average bunch—but no lead was given them—no daily bulletin—no encouragement.—Sleep, with an easy heart.

Friday November 2 1923

Very cold night last night: extra cold this morning.—S. K. along after breakfast, very excited & nervous. 'Give me that,' he said (meaning the packet of MS.) I gave it to him. In about 5 minutes he returned, smiling. 'It's gone,' he said. 'Well that's a load off my chest. He'll bring me the receipt tomorrow' he said. 'Have you the other?' 'I have; but it's broken up and distributed among my clothes.' 'Make it up; I'll get it out tomorrow.' 'But I've no sealing wax.' 'I've some—Sheela's. See how useful everything proves in the long run'.—After lock-up I retrieved the 3 separate packets from sleeves & back of coat & made them up into neat packet as before, sealing it on my bed. Hope good luck will attend them after so many hairbreadth 'scapes in the deadly imminent raid.

Sat. November 3 1923

S.K. along with receipt for packet yesterday. 'No 330. Certificate of posting a Registered Postal Packet. Mrs. Campbell Lackandarragh Enniskerry, Co Wicklow.' Postmark 'Droichead Nua Co. Chille Dara 2 No. 23'. Took out 2nd one. A load off my chest.—S. K. very cheerful—in top of his form. 'Don't boast. We're not out of the wood yet. They may be opened in the Post Office. You can congratulate me when you get a letter from your wife saying that they have arrived safely. I wonder will the fact of 2 packets arriving more or less together—after the hunger-strike too,—attract suspicion.'—About 5.30 p.m. (sitting round stove—very cold and damp dusk falling outside) a strange prisoner came along. 'Tom Longmore wd. like to see you. He's in No 16 hospital'. Went over. Figures of prisoners moving about in cold darkness. Electric lights of compound white & repellent. Knocked at hospital door. No response. Lifted latch by inserting my knife. Hospital interior gloomy and *cold*—much colder than 12 Hut. No friendly glimmer of stove. As I passed down the hut looking for T. L. (didn't know location of bed) was stopped by Fr. Daly's weak voice from R. side. 'Hello, Joe.' Talked with him—oh, the smell. Human foetor—sheets & bedding unchanged. Down to T. L. (3 or 4 beds down same side). T. L. ditto—horrid smell. Muffler round neck—glands swollen—voice very weak. Had to stoop down to hear him. 'I'd like an American paper, if you've one.' (Gave him one which I had brought over). Taking food. Release promised thro' instrumentality of a former Dep. Governor (Duffy) & Sean MacGarry.[99] All these releases worked by influence. Back to Hut 12—nausea & disillusionment, 'I wouldn't like any of my friends to be like that, or any of my friends to see me like that. Hunger-strike?—never again'.

Sunday 4 November 1923

Out in the sun before breakfast S. K. spoke of the rats having deserted Hut 5. 'They have not been about these last few nights.' I said: 'They have deserted Hut 12 too. Before the hunger-strike & for the first 2 or 3 nights of it they kept gnawing all the time. I was afraid of them—afraid lest they might attack us when we grew real weak. They went off to the cakes in the trench opposite 18 Hut, I think.' 'But would they eat them all? I doubt it; they'd only nibble at them here & there. I wasn't over there, so don't know. Did you ever hear of the rat in West Kerry that came every night & sucked the breast of a young married woman? Her husband did his best to banish it—went to the priest, said special prayers—but all to no purpose. The woman was a very good woman too. The people talked about it, but not openly. Nobody liked to, about Dunquin. At last it became so bad that the husband sold out & bought a farm 40 miles away in the Killarney direction. But the rat followed them there. I don't know what became of the woman: we lost track of her when she left our part of the country'.—Fine bracing sunny day. No football—none since the strike ended. There are about 50 men still on strike. I went over to the Hospital with papers for Frank Daly. Looking very weak—yellow waxen skin—eyes yellowish & appealing. In a weak voice, he said: 'I had a bad night last night. That adjutant-doctor—Boland—wanted to give me an injection but I wouldn't let him. I'll take nothing until I get my unconditional release'. 'They'll let you go as far as it is safe before they release you Frank. I wonder they don't let you out on account of your brother.' 'That doesn't count,' said Frank. 'Without a brother in the F. S. I'd be better off'. After this morning's and last night's experience—seeing these men Tom Longmore & Frank Daly & others—lying weak & neglected—smelling, so that their nearest & dearest would run away from them—I'm convinced that a hunger-strike is not worthwhile. The cost is too great; the conditions too bad, the value set on human life or on mere humanitarianism too trifling in Ireland today. As a race we ought to be ashamed of ourselves. We have, at the best, nothing to be proud of. And we set such store by ourselves—a race of vipers & hypocrites.' Read article in Philadelphia Public Ledger on D'Annunzio & his women-folk. I like the outspokenness of American yellow journalism. It's better than the dreary suggestion & morbidity of papers like *The News of the World* or *Lloyd's News*—or the Sunday Independent. Their cosmopolitanism, too, is exciting. Imagine if there was a depôt opened for the sale of foreign papers & books in Dublin they wd. meet with a ready sale.

[The main events of November after the strike included the capture of a letter from the Camp O/C, Christy Byrne, about the hunger-strike, a Free State Propaganda coup. 'Old' Jack Keogh's son's capture (after the news of his shooting proved false) was reported on 8 November 1923. New prisoners arrived on 10 November. There was talk of a large number of releases.]

Monday 5 November 1923

Hard frost last night. Out before breakfast the air was like wine—country looked clean & sunny the trees swathed in mist—the Wicklow Hills obliterated in great drifts of white & blue fog. Yellow coal smoke curling from pipes over roof of huts. Said S. K. 'This hard dry cold suits me. Like American cold. It's the raw damp that does for me.' Rumor of 150 releases from Tintown 3.—About 3 p.m. S.K. came in: 'I've a rumor. The Cabinet has met & we're all to be released before Christmas. The breadman shouted it across the wires. Are you pulling my leg? No, says he.—I'd like to get out for Christmas.' 'We may eat our Christmas dinner in Lackan, Seán. Think of it—turkey, wine etc—& freedom!' No letters since I wrote on Monday week (end of strike). No parcels. The Censors must be holding up letters.—After lights out Socko & 2 P. A.'s in (very suddenly & quietly). 'Get into your beds!' A fellow let a great fart. 'Socko!' 'Work it up you!' said Socko.

Thursday 22 November 1923

Heavy night's frost again—very cold. The gulls do not prance & rattle on roof now. Where have they gone? Third day of Curragh races—will frost interfere? Fog, fog, as yesterday: white, throaty, penetrating, Cooks called out early (as per yesterday's notice) for early breakfast. To facilitate releases? P.A. in in dark—impediment in speech:—'Wh-e-r-re's the cook?' Light switched on. Cooks go out etc. in dark. Up 7.30 a.m. in expectation of draft going today. Frost, post outside. All taps in washhouse frozen—for first time. Over to sand-bank opposite Black House to get grease & carbon deposit off utensils. Foggy sentry (*always* the sentry): frozen gulls; frozen cakes of sand; frost white on barbed wires—like frost on thorny sprays of a country hedge. Hands frozen & tingling.—Very few releases. 3 out of Hut 12—one of them Muirís Breathnach of Listowel. Shook hands: '*Go n-éirighidh do bhóthar leat!* ['Good luck!'—literally, 'May the road rise with you!'] Always emotional with a Gael. Conny Ryan to fore carrying out beds—which *will* stick in back door. Have a 'hunch' today that I will be held over Xmas with 3000 men. Where will be our place of detention?—Shaved with difficulty owing to cold & men coming & going.—Rocky in. The Govt. will *not* hand over the body of Denis Barry[100] or of any other man dying on hunger-strike. Christian burial promised. Dick Mulcahy doesn't want public demonstrations—which may cause further deaths outside & inside. Inquest on Barry held. Coroner & jury wish body handed over, but G. H. Q. puts ban on it. Body may be handed over later when public safety is not menaced. Discussion round stove: 'Everything the F.S. does now it does wrong. Forced into impossible position. No precedent for holding body of prisoner not executed. Even convicts handed over to relatives. Legality?' 'But they know no law.' 'Except the *Lex salus populi* [Law of public safety]' says T. Campbell[101] from bed.—T. C. has been laid up with a cold. His faithful brother (so like, so unlike him) to & fro with food parcels etc. Tommy listens to us (unapprovingly—Catholic Puritan) talk about Garibaldi & Roman Republic of 1849, & subsequent movement. Old Jack Keogh at stove (back to cold back-door) on history of Catholic Church in Ireland. Strongbow's time—Sir Felim O'Neill 1641—Rinuccini—Owen Roe only leader that ever led an Irish army—Sarsfield[102]—Pepys' references to Irish Catholiques. George III and America. Rip Van Winkle. 'Farmer George' of Windsor (Thackeray). Dean Swift. Only a foreigner could lead an Irish army etc. (As I write this insects eating me: close to forms with prisoners talking round stove ('revolvers'—'Ballina'—'armoured car'—snatches of talk—arm of Western prisoner, gesticulating, jostles me—the 'sh' sound of western speech—'g's' at ends of words—'ing' pronounced carefully). Shinners reading aloud from St. Anthony's—Catholic magazine (came in my parcel—handed to him as edifying reading) about Prophecies of S. Malachy. Letters in: One handed to me by Seán Mooney—'Here, Joseph!'—from N. dated Sunday 18/Nov/23 (quote).—Rocky says it's a heartbreak to go into Hut 15 now. One of the Considines is off the strike. Only about 30 men on now. Billy Walsh means business—it's a death sentence. Seán Twomey still pink. Hut 15 cheerless, cold. Lemon drink between P. Cahill T. D. & B. Walsh frozen into solid block of ice. This will give you an idea of the temperature of the hut. Tom Dennehy & orderlies doing their best to keep place clean etc.—2.30 p.m. Visitors, man & woman, for one of the far-gone strikers. What do they think of the grey, muddy, frosty, cheerless Tintown? A sad place to die. Will bodies be dumped in compound—trench—or removed to Mountjoy beside Rory O'Connor etc.—C. Byrne stops to talk to me & P. Landers. ('Shit, or get off the pot.' 'That's d—d good—the Govt. shit or get off etc.' 'Seán a chóta makes me laugh'.) I haven't talked to C. B. since failure of strike. He offers me tobacco from pouch—have none, so take it—Maltan Flake. C. B.'s method of pacification—a sop.—Walk after dinner in cold foggy air with S. K. 'I was nearly caught talking to H&E & Kelly in Hut 18. It's out of bounds—but what's a fellow to do? I may get out one of these nights. They'd leave me beyond the gate & let me take my chance.' S. K. pale & chesty. 'The damned place doesn't agree with me. None of my letters have got out lately. No reply from Sheela.[103] No parcel from Nurse Cahill etc.' May try & get out a selection of MSS tomorrow. Shall I register it? Or not? fortunes of war; element of luck in life. Worrying over release: heavy kit-bags: degradation of search: no money.—My name called out by Jack Staunton: 'Joe Campbell'—parcel from N. *No* condensed milk, but have got a tin of brown polish at last.—After lock up, G. Wallace tells us that he is promoted to Camp Orderly Officer. Chaffing by men on forms round stove 4. George tells mysteriously of some arrangement between Sinn Féin H.Q. & F. S. over calling-off of hunger-strike. Not very communicative, when I try to draw him. The *careful* old soldier. Describe his face & slow speech—or lack of speech. 'Will there be a public guarantee of release by Xmas?' Does *not* answer. A character.—I am confident & *not* confident of eating my Xmas dinner at home. Wish the tension was over. After supper, discussion on conference & treaty. Griffith's character & death.

Friday 23 November 1923

As we were told last night after parade for count that all men in bed in the morning wd. be forced to go to Hospital if not astir for morning count, all men were up early this morning.—Greasy cook in by back door before count & told us that the Hunger-Strike was declared off in all jails & camps. Tom Derrig & 'Seumas' Robinson[104] were in this camp at 2 o'c this morning. Came down by Govt. motor from the Joy. We discussed it. Was Seumas Robinson a prisoner? Never heard of his capture. Was he working with prisoners in 'Joy from outside? Some agreement must have been come to between Republicans & Staters. Out to sand-heap of trench opp. Black House to scrape my mug & plate. Does anybody live in this house? all signs of habitation, but never saw anybody leaving it or entering it. White hoar frost again. No fog. It was bitterly cold all night.—Several prisoners over to Hut 15 to see men off strike. Billy Walsh in great form. Reprieve from death-sentence.—About 10 a.m. the 22 men off strike were carried by prisoners & P. A.'s to Hospital 16. 3 cases removed to Curragh Hospital. Men on hunger-strike 35 days—some Mtjoy men 5 days more. Wylie of Waterford, it seems, broke off a few hours before Derrig's & Robinson's arrival, but he gets on all sides great credit for stand. (He was moved back from Curragh, one remembers). He went off strike after visit of sister & brother-in-law the other day.—S. K. in. Critical, as usual. He says the strike is off 'unconditionally'. No negotiations took place. Sold again by amateur leadership?—Beautiful hard sunshiny day with frost underfoot—melting in *warm* sun. Compound still white all over. Walked briskly in air. Confident of release before Xmas—with a secret gnawing heart-pang of uncertainty. At stove 4, Tommy McPhillips the little brown-coated Monaghan man says: 'The suspense is a terror. I'd rather do 5 years, & know when I was going to be released, than suffer on in this way.'—A few releases out of Hut 12. Kit MacNamara released—his appearance & character. A shopkeeper, or shop boy? General 'flouriness'. More room now for my bed. Very congested up till this.—Talk around Stove 4 of Cockfights. Otters. Badgers. Describe at length. The birds plucked all but neck & wings. Steel spur made by blacksmith, Birds fight in *air*. Rounds—rubbing etc. If winning cock does not attack 'dead' cock after knock-out, not counted game. Piles of notes on ground with stone weighting them to prevent them being blown away. Describe at length. I keep thinking that this is Saturday. Feeling of days. Fry rashers for dinner. No heed paid now to customs of Church. Why should *we* fast?—Letter from N. dated Sunday 18/xi/23. (quote) (Was this yesterday?)—Depression. Reaction follows hope of morning. Hunger-strikers after first great relief at deliverance from death will, in a day or two, brood over failure. They may not be released, after all.—2.30 p.m. While copying MS. of diary, S. K. & Paddy Landers in. The day's paper does not confirm Derrig's visit, they say. K. O'Higgins[105] in a die-hard mood. S. K. went off to get paper. Returned with it (he is great at *getting* things) & read it. (Quote O'Higgins) Inquest on Denis Barry. Inquest on Derham T.D. who fell down stairs of Spicer's pub in Balbriggan & cracked his skull. Photograph in other day's paper—unpleasant drooped eyelids & open mouth. Our T.D.'s—who voted for Treaty. Low types: boosting in corrupt press. 'Amidst heavy snow & frost farmers in Tyrone are cutting the corn crop.' Ulster Players programme for Gaiety Theatre next week—the same old thing. As I read in came Seán Healy. Describe sneaky appearance. Why is it that I don't like most Corkmen? Broaches subject of paper.—'Have you a copy of the paper was published in the Joy?' 'Doesn't sound like release, does it.' Annoyed—'chawed him off.' Went off: 'that's not the spirit'—threat. etc. etc. Nothing more to do with life of camp except observe, observe, observe. Out in air for walk. The sound of a fiddle playing a reel in Hut 2. First time since Hunger-strike.—Before 'count' (after lock-up) read the day's *Freeman's Journal* to assembled crowd round stove 4. Crowd from other sections listens—Sean O'Farrell (grave & intelligent as always), Honan etc. Some prisoners take a great interest in news: others none at all. Comment of Councillor of Athy No 1 R. D. C. on inordinately heavy sentences & fines imposed by District Justices. Are these sentences pre-arranged? The heavy hand of Govt? F. S. loan launched by E. Blythe at Dublin Chamber of Commerce. The Unionist crowd present. List of names—names always interesting. Waterford Co. Council £57000 in debt: outstanding rates (assets) £9000. Borrowing £30000 from Govt.—Meeting in Mansion House re Dependents of 6 Counties Internees. P. T. McGinley, Fr. Fullerton's strong ironic speaking. National soldier courtmartialled for taking a letter out for a prisoner in the 'Joy. S. K. greatly interested as it concerns him. I remember he drew my attention to it earlier, but I wasn't listening very attentively.—Supper of rashers and tea. Seán Mooney bawling at top of voice. Jack White's comments: 'He makes more noise than all the men in the hut put together.' Rocky silent & full of wisdom. Upper lip more curved than usual. Hands joined between close knees. Head bent over fire.—I write these notes on knee in very bad light.

S. Mooney is bawling again. 'It'll break some of your hearts to hear your numbers called out. Why the hell don't ye get back from the fire, and let somebody else warm his shins before he gets into bed? No more heat from the warm stove! etc. etc.' Then in the bookmaker's voice:—'Six to four the field! Six to four the field! What price you carry the old box out in the morning, George?'—Tommy Campbell (in bed with cold)—peculiar voice—speaking bad Irish *plus* English to Eugene Swiney of Dundalk. The latter's ponderosity and Fainne[106] Ring. I always suspect people with labels—Fainne's, temperance badges, feminist badges etc. We're a queer race.—Read 'On Tolstoi & other things' in November number of *Adelphi* by Middleton Murry (quote).—As I finish writing these notes Cosgrave is sweeping, & raising a dust. I hate dust. What will the morning bring? Release? *Not* freezing as I finish. Must go to bed.

[On 24 November 1923 he remarks 'There are only 81 men in Hut 12 now, About 1100 in Camp 2. Never so low before. Only 43 of the original men who came in from 'Joy on 20 February 1923'. Stuart was released, as was 'old man' Keogh. Subjects of conversations include 'we are not a chosen people—we never produced a Rembrandt'; criticism of Red Cross; refusal of Bishop of Cork to allow Denis Barry Christian burial.]

Sat 1 December 1923

Drear-hearted December! Another December in jail. Fine morning. Frost. Wraith of sun (very bright & spirit-like) doing its best to pierce a *thin* white fog, obscuring everything. Not thick fog; *very* thin

& gossamery.—Rice for breakfast—as thin as the fog; tasting of the sacks & dust of the loft wherever stored.—10 a.m. Wicklow Hills faint lilac; mist dispersed. 11 a.m. Wicklow Hills clear & resplendent, covered with snow. Fairy hills. White on northerly spur of North Prison of Lugnacullia very clear & cold. Valleys marked distinctly in the sunlight.—Letter from N. dated 27/XI/23 enclosing one from Carrie Townshend about W. B. Y.'s & Æ's joint application for my release.[107] Talked it over with S. K. (he's been very seedy these last few days, but is greatly bucked this morning owing to having received acknowledgement of MS of his Gaelic diary from Sheela of Kilmallock.) My ironic remarks on Yeats & Æ. Says Seán 'They've shit on their pants, & now they're doing their best to pretend that they haven't.' Jack Staunton of Westport is taken out by Kennedy to office. K asked me what hut he was in. I said '12—my hut.' After some time he returns, laughing:—'It was for interrogation. They asked me would I leave the country. They'd pay my passage to Canada if I'd go.' 'They'd like to get us all out—so as to make Ireland a happy hunting-ground for Free State placemen. But we'll stay—& our children will stay after us.'—3 p.m. Rocky & Tom Kelly are arrested by Windy Joe for talking across wires to a friend in Camp 1.—Later: Rocky is back. Surrounded by crowd anxious to hear his experience. Lip curved: eyes bulging—wise, humorous look on excited face. Was brought before Dep. Gov. Prendergast. Lecture: 'Owing to the near approach of Christmas you'll be let off this time. But any other time it wd. have meant the Glasshouse.' (Ugh!) 'You know what the Glasshouse is.' He describes Windy Joe—'the bastard.' Connie Ryan is in crowd—& Con Leahy the lame prisoner wounded in the Glen of Aherlow with Denny Lacy.[108] His shock head of black curly hair—smiles, as a big man smiles, showing good teeth—leaning pathetically on sticks.—Bad coal in stove. Comfortless fire, & we want a *good* one. *Mí-ádh* [Bad luck] on Irish things. Burn everything English but their coal!? After count the Hut o/c intimates that Camp Commdt. requires prisoners to stand to their beds in the morning. If not the Governor will take necessary steps to get men out of bed. etc.

[Early December: Talk at stove of Glasshouse & its horrors—'they kick the shite out of you'. 'Amusing Delvin—Brinsley MacNamara—case.'[109] *'4955 prisoners still in (Govt. figures)'.]*

Friday 7 December 1923

Desperate rain in small hours of morning. Confiners rattle on iron roof. Back door opened. Wet & stormy. Shirts etc. on line flapping desolately in wind. Wind from South. Not cold. Dash for breakfast in whirling rain. Pools of muddy water splashing in face as prisoners run. Floor of Dining Hall 6 wet—water running along channels to take off horse urine—windows broken, or altogether frameless—drifts of rain blowing in on dirty tables—drip, drip from roof—down one's neck etc. (It was in these Dining Halls the first of the hunger strike-breakers were housed—luckily it was dry then). Cocoa for breakfast. Why cocoa? Buckshee store? Or is some contractor, or Senator profiting by it? 'It's to make us fat for release,' said Seán Mooney. 'Convicts always get it before release to get them into condition for going out etc.' Huddled round stove 4 with other prisoners (brooding—cannot read) S. K. in. *'Lá fliuch a Seáin.' 'Lá fliuch, agus lá salach agus lá suaireach, agus –'* ['A wet day, Seán.' 'Wet and dirty and miserable and –'] 'The only thing for it on a day like this is *leaba agus buidéal.' 'Agus Jane!'* [bed and a bottle.' 'And a Jane!'] said S. K. stalking out. Men amused.—Letters in; but none for me.—Copied notes for diary. S. K. along again as I write. He's received a letter from Mary Hussey. Over to Dining Hall 7 to read it. Encounter with Toomey, Lord Dunsany's[110] woodranger etc. Tall, soldier-like, full of talk & ingenuous frankness. A likeable man. My daughter—15. Lord D. gives her my wages every week. Sends me (per grocer) 1£ worth of parcel every week. Educated my son—a compositor in *Irish Times* office. Loyalty of man to master. He comments on Lord D's eccentricity. Old clothes, patched & darned. Old boots—the incident with the Cockney valet & the bull terrier pup which ate a piece out of the back of one of the boots. Explanations. Advice of Toomey to Cockney valet as to how to humour the Lord. Threw pairs of old stockings on to dungheap. 'My father's stockings etc.' Toomey keeps laces, safety pins, horseshoe nails in pockets to patch up Lord D's clothes when out shooting or going over estate. Great poet & playwright. LEDWIDGE OF SLANE.[111] DOESN'T BOTHER WITH SOCIETY—LORD JERSEY'S DAUGHTER. In detention with Lord D. over ammunition in B[lack] & T[an] times. Lord D. wouldn't have guard on house. Sorrow for Sir Horace Plunkett's house[112] being burned. 'They'll burn this place next.' Sir John Dillon's house– 1 mile away—blown up. 'You could hear the explosion over ten miles of countryside.' Offered 6000£ to leader of raiders to spare mansion, but they had to carry out orders. Not a car was taken on Lord D. The Staters came to suspect that somebody in Lord Dunsany's service was in the confidence of the I.R.A. & I was arrested. etc. etc.—Tea.—Parcels in. Found bundle of papers on bed from Joe Judge, Phila.—N. Y. Times Magazine Section, Phila. Public Ledger, N. Y. Times Bk. Reviews etc. Looked at pictures in Times Magazine: Trouble on the Rhine—the Rhenish Republic—uniformed troops for all the world like Irish Irregulars. Similarity of humans of different races. Holds-up in streets—'sky them'—searches. Mussolini at an anniversary parade of the Fascisti in Rome—looks like Napoleon—thrust out lips—rather fancies himself as Dictator. Article on Hunger-Strike (hostile) in *Phila. Public Ledger*. Release, it says, for Xmas; but Dev. will be kept in. Attack on Cuban administration; conditions very like those of F. S.—graft, nepotism etc. Free State Hangman (quote). Logue on Prisoners.[113] Article on Lincoln's speech at Gettysburg. Did Pearse model his oratory on Lincoln's style? Analogy.—S. K. in before lock-up. Gave me cigarettes. I gave him Hovis loaf & butter. No success, so far with H & E. (instalment of diary). May get out letter tonight. Have no stamps to write Xmas letters.

9 p.m. Supper over. Sean Mooney chanting 'Yes, we've no Bananas.' Chorus! Prisoners (with light from blazing fire on papers & faces, or backs of heads & shoulders—some are sitting with their backs towards me, where I write on my bed) looking at N. Y. Times pictures. (They *love* pictures). Eugene Sweeney—Fáinne—baldish temples (only a young man) with Gaelic book—toothbrush moustache pursed out—

very solemn—a character. Aleck MacMahon puffing with smacking lips at his old pipe which is plugged up. Magennis bent two-double over a dog-eared copy of 'Won on the Turf' (Magennis is always in a stooping posture). T. Campbell on his bed on other side of stove fingering at the strings of his violin. Jack White with novel, in shadow against electric light bulb & firelight—leaning back on [*illegible*] post—cap on head—glasses—pallor—light reflected on pages of open book. G. Wallace talking to his Limerick friends—Enright & Maloney from Pallas—deep Munster brogue. Sound of beds being pulled out for making down. Red glow from open door of Stove 3—all fires burning well tonight. Clothes hanging on lines overhead. Wet floor of hut shining in light from fires etc. All cold gone—very close. Whether the result of weather—or of cocoa—or of both combined—feeling a bit seedy. Dirty, too. No bath for months. Jack White says 'I see in the papers Yeats is going to Stockholm to get the Nobel Prize.' 'His bank balance will be a little fatter for that.' 'He looks very dreamy-looking,' said a Milltown prisoner. 'Dreamy in look maybe—but there's no better businessman than Yeats. A regular moneygrub.' Spoke of his pensions from British Civil list, marriage etc.—Mass in morning: a holiday. 'No releases tomorrow on a/c of holiday.'—Corky Ryan has gone to bed early. He is asleep—pale, dead looking face.

[Entries discussing the prospect of release. 'Influence of racing crowd that worked Billy Walsh's release, More powerful with Cabinet than of Dunsany, or Gogarty or W.B.Y. or Æ. Is Lord Powerscourt working against me? D. Fitzgerald's influence nil. "Mabel", says Seán Kavanagh 'would like to get you out of course, she's ashamed when she meets Nancy. Letter of Yeats & AE might do you more harm than good." Kavanagh gets news: 'Going in the morning. My name is on the list.]

Sunday 16 December 1923

Bathed at tap in washhouse—very cold. Prisoners think me mad!

Controversy among men returned from Mass. Priest preached on John the Baptist. 'A great man' 'not clothed in soft garments.' De

Valera—'I will strip him of his sainthood'. Petty men in disturbed times. Toomey from latrine greets me. 'Great county for spuds,' says Dundalk man. 'Great county for holding prisoners—for taming lions & tigers & bad boys—boys their mothers never would have tamed.'

Will turkey & geese be cooked on Bacilikill stove at Xmas? Workhouse fare—½ quarter of tobacco—less than normal fare for prisoners—cooks will not cook. Notice up on cook-house door: 2 letters may be sent out week ending 22nd Dec. Means few releases. *I* am not confident that I will be released.

Search in Huts for confessional-box. All out except men in bed. Got on prisoner—'got it from a man released'.

Wonderful sky over compound—great masses of black-blue cloud overhead—with vivid sunlight penetrating through gaps—edges lit up—pearl white & silvery along south & west horizon, full of light.—Wicklow Hills obscured by great banks of snowy & violet & silver cumulus. Air soft—green Xmas. String of horses from Parkinson's stable out—unusual to see them exercising on Sunday. Turf must be very springy. Brown muddy compound, like winter ploughed field. Green musketry ranges & exercise fields beyond. Eternal blockhouse & wire.

Tim Healy leader of minority-majority. K. O'Higgins & Dev. & Einstein. Over jorums of Whisky & soda in Viceregal Lodge coin phrases—well-taught by Tim Healy.

MUGS OF BLOOD

Silver band taken from priest's umbrella. Chalice next. George Wallace.

P Landers in & Dr Comer at stove. Stories of Seán a Chóta—his erratic restless character—easily misunderstood—warm-hearted etc. & as simple as a child. His love of Nature. Where is he? Walking round Sley head gazing over Atlantic? or in Dunleary with Jane? Landers story of getting the book & the seats taken on him. H. Johnston in (bearded & foreign—waxen face—red lips). Story of capture of Dundalk by Irregulars.

Plan to make potyeen in Hut for Xmas. Right under Staters' nose. Potyeen priests. The ex-army chaplain told of by T. Campbell. How to make a still by Jem Mulholland. Pope Mullarkey. The tinsmith whose trade was still making—horns & worms & arms—sugar & molasses, barley malt, yeast—'woeful smell' Tintown Potstill. Fine matured Irregular. Release in morning?

The Tintown diary ends here.

Notes to Introduction

1 The only biography of Campbell is by Norah Saunders and A. A. Kelly, *Joseph Campbell: Poet & Nationalist 1879–1944* (Dublin, 1988). A number of autobiographical broadcasts made by Campbell late in his life, with the general title 'A Northern Autobiography', are reprinted in *Journal of Irish Literature*, VIII, 3 (September, 1979), Joseph Campbell special issue, edited by Sr. Assumpta Saunders, pp.60–96.
2 'A Northern Autobiography', pp. 60, 65.
3 Joseph Campbell, *Poems* (ed. with an introduction by Austin Clarke, Dublin, 1963), p. 9.
4 *Poems*, p. 93.
5 Austin Clarke, 'Joseph Campbell: A personal sketch and a critical assessment' in *Journal of Irish Literature*, VIII, 3 (1979), pp. 24, 23.
6 See Campbell's account of his political activities at this time, written in 1942 when he applied for a military pension from De Valera's government (it was refused). This account makes it possible to explain some of the diary's more cryptic references to the events of this period: TCD, MS 10202/1312–1324.
7 TCD, MS 10202/1321.
8 Nickname of a camp guard.
9 C. S. Andrews, *Dublin Made Me* (Dublin and Cork, 1979), p. 299.
10 Ballykinlar, Co. Down.

Notes to Narrative

1 Parody of a popular song, 'Bewitched, bothered and bewildered' from a musical, *Pal Joey*.
2 Robert Barton (1881–1975), TD for Wicklow and cousin of Erskine Childers (see below, note 18). He had been one of the signatories of the Anglo-Irish Treaty but later campaigned against its acceptance. Brigade staff officer, Dublin Brigade, during the fighting in the city in June–July.
3 Date of attempted escape by Republicans in Mountjoy.
4 Dr James Ryan (1891–1970), TD for Wexford. Had established a temporary hospital inside the Four Courts. Captured after its fall. Cell-mate of Campbell for a time in Mountjoy.
5 Peadar Breslin, who had fought in the Four Courts.
6 Liam Mellows (1892–1922) had fought in Galway and travelled to America on Volunteer business during the War of Independence. Was one of the Four Courts garrison. Executed in Mountjoy on 8 December; see below, note 29.

7 Had fought the British in Kerry. Commandant 1st Eastern Division with HQ in Drogheda. Organiser of escape attempt from Mountjoy.

8 *'Póilín Airm'*: Military Policeman.

9 Perhaps Frank Gallagher (1898–1962), who wrote underground propaganda in War of Independence and Civil War. He was in Mountjoy in 1922.

10 Art O'Connor had been a leader of the Republican resistance in Dublin which held out for five days in O'Connell Street after the surrender of the Four Courts on 30 June 1922.

11 George Gavan Duffy (1882–1951), Dáil Minister for Foreign Affairs from January to July 1922.

12 Oliver Gogarty (1878–1957), poet and surgeon, was shortly to be a Senator.

13 Presumably the deaths of Arthur Griffith (of a cerebral haemorrhage) and Michael Collins (in an ambush at Béal na mBláth) on 12 and 22 August, 1922. Gogarty had embalmed Collins's body.

14 Renvyle, Gogarty's house in Co. Galway, was burned on 23 February 1923.

15 'Paudeen' O'Keeffe, Deputy Governor of Mountjoy, had been general secretary of Sinn Féin 1913–22 and had himself been imprisoned in Richmond Barracks in Dublin in 1916.

16 This was the address of Desmond (1888–1947) and Mabel FitzGerald. He was Minister for External Affairs while she had strong Republican sympathies.

17 These were the first executions of prisoners under the Army's proclamation of 10 October 1922, providing for the death penalty for those found in possession of arms.

18 Erskine Childers (1870–1922) organised importation of arms for the Irish Volunteers in July 1914 in the yacht *Asgard*. Director of Propaganda for Dáil Éireann, later for anti-Treaty side. Captured on 10 November 1922 at Glendalough House, home of his cousin Robert Barton. Tried and condemned for possession of a revolver, the gift of Michael Collins. Executed November 24.

19 Captured with Childers on 10 November 1922.

20 Thomas Johnson (1872–1963), leader of the Labour Party. In fact he opposed the executions. See J. Anthony Gaughan, *Thomas Johnson, 1872–1963, First Leader of the Labour Party in Dáil Éireann* (Dublin, 1980), p. 218.

21 Reference to the seventeenth-century witch-craze, which led to several accusations of witchcraft, and to trials and executions, in the town of Salem, Massachusetts.

22 Anthology in which poems of Campbell's appeared.

23 The Plan of Campaign was a strategy adopted by tenant leaders in 1886–7 during the Land War. Tenants on certain estates offered their landlords what their organisation regarded as a 'fair rent.' The Plan was declared unlawful on 18 December 1886 and repressive measures followed.

24 The Anglo-Irish Treaty, signed on 6 December 1921.
25 Dublin Metropolitan Police, amalgamated with the Gárda Síochána in 1925.
26 See note 24 above.
27 David Lloyd George (1863–1945), British Prime Minister at the time of the signing of the Treaty.
28 Seán Hales (1890–1922) was a Free State Major-General and TD for West Cork. Pádraig Ó Máille was Leas-cheann comhairle (Deputy Speaker) of the Dáil.
29 Rory O'Connor (1883–1922), Liam Mellows, Joe McKelvey and Richard Barrett had all been prominent members of the Four Courts garrison which had surrendered on 30 June 1922.
30 *Hamlet,* Act III Scene 1.
31 Kevin Roantree O'Shiel (1891–1970), legal secretary to the Provisional Government, after Collins's death appointed director of the North Eastern Boundary Bureau.
32 Pádraic Ó Conaire (1882–1928), perhaps the most distinguished Gaelic writer of the day.
33 Robert Stewart, Viscount Castlereagh and 2nd Marquess of Londonderry (1769–1822), remembered in Ireland as a Chief Secretary who campaigned for the Union with Britain, was attacked by Shelley in his poem *The Mask of Anarchy.*
34 Padraic Colum (1881–1972), Irish poet and writer, a friend of Campbell's for many years who had emigrated to the United States in 1914.
35 Special Constabulary, founded in 1920 'to assist the authorities in the maintenance of order', in theory anywhere in Ireland but in practice in the six counties from which Northern Ireland was formed in 1921.
36 Simon Donnelly had escaped from Kilmainham Jail in 1921 with Ernie O'Malley (see below, note 47). A member of the Four Courts garrison.
37 Kevin Barry (1902–1920), executed 1 November 1920; Patrick Moran, executed 14 March 1921; Thomas Whelan, executed 14 March 1921.
38 William Carleton (1794–1869), fiction writer from Co. Tyrone, who wrote on rural themes.
39 James Larkin (1876–1947), founder of the Irish Transport and General Workers' Union in 1909, had gone to America in 1914, been arrested for his left-wing activities and sentenced to five to ten years in prison in 1920. He was pardoned in January 1923 and returned to Ireland in April of that year.
40 The *Freeman's Journal*, Dublin (1763–1923) supported the Treaty.
41 The armoured car was originally named the *Ballinalee* but was renamed after its capture by Republicans on 13 July 1922. Recaptured by Free State forces on 20 September. See O'Farrell, *Who's Who,* p. 142, Hopkinson, *Green Against Green,* p. 159.
42 Sister Angela was a member of the Bon Secours order of nuns. She is said to have smuggled comforts to political prisoners.

43 Seán Óg Ó Caomhánaigh (1885–1946) also known as Seán Kavanagh, Seán a'chóta: Irish scholar, from Dunquin, Co. Kerry. The nickname 'Seán a' chóta' means 'of the petticoat', and may be an allusion to his having been kept in girl's clothing as was the custom for small boys in Gaeltacht areas, but longer than was customary.

44 May refer to Walter Starkie (1894–1976), linguist and literary man, later Professor of Spanish at Trinity College, Dublin, or to James Sullivan Starkey (1897–1958), founder of the *Dublin Magazine*, who wrote under the name of Seumas O'Sullivan.

45 Internment camp in Co. Down.

46 Joe McGarritty (1874–1940), Clan na Gael (Irish-American) leader, fund-raiser for Dáil Éireann during War of Independence. Dr Patrick McCartan (1878–1966), sent as Irish envoy to Washington by Dáil Éireann in 1919.

47 Ernie O'Malley (1898–1957), organiser of countrywide military activity in War of Independence, later author of the classic account of the period, *On Another Man's Wound* (London, 1932); escaped after Four Courts surrender; recaptured and imprisoned in Mountjoy, November 1922. Peadar O'Donnell (1893–1986), writer, socialist agitator and commander of Donegal West Brigade, fought in Four Courts. Michael Kilroy, Commandant 4th Western Division, captured September 1922.

48 H. Francis Stuart (1902–2000), married to Maud Gonne MacBride's natural daughter Iseult; he had been imprisoned in Portlaoise (then Maryboro') prison which he and others had burned. Poet, later a novelist whose *Black List, Section H* (Carbondale, Ill., 1971) describes some of the same events as Campbell's diary.

49 Liam Lynch (1893–1923), Commandant of the 1st Southern Division, the most important Republican military leader still at large.

50 Later O/C of the prisoners in the Camp.

51 Humphrey Murphy and Dan Breen, respectively Republican commanders in North Kerry and Tipperary. Breen was captured shortly after the death of Liam Lynch, while Murphy remained at large until after the ceasefire of 24 May, and de Valera was arrested when he came out of hiding to address a meeting in Ennis on 15 August. (Hopkinson, *Green Against Green*, pp. 238, 257, 261.)

52 Constance Markievicz (1868–1927), née Gore-Booth, Labour leader, officer in Irish Citizen Army and first woman elected to House of Commons; she opposed the Treaty.

53 P. J. Ruttledge (1892–1952), Republican politician, TD for Mayo, member of de Valera's Republican cabinet and later his deputy.

54 Internment camp in Co. Meath.

55 Countess Markievicz.

56 William Bulfin (1864–1910), friend of Arthur Griffith, author of *Rambles in Eirinn* (1907), had worked as a gaucho in Argentina and run a periodical called *The Southern Cross*. His daughter later married Seán MacBride; see note 61 below.

57 Laurence Ginnell (1854–1923), anti-Treaty TD.

58 C. K. Shorter, English editor and critic married to the Irish poet Dora Sigerson (1866–1918). Louise Imogen Guiney, Catholic scholar and writer.

59 Austin Stack (1880–1929), leading anti-Treaty politician and TD for Kerry and West Limerick, captured April 1923. Denny Lacy, Tipperary guerilla killed February 1923. Sir Roger Casement (1864–1916), British colonial administrator until 1912 and later international organiser for Irish Volunteers, captured on landing from a German submarine at Easter 1916 at Banna Strand, Co. Kerry; tried and executed.

60 Bruree and Kilmallock are towns in Co. Limerick. The Republicans held out in Munster between June and August 1922, until Government forces took Cork and Tralee by sea and turned their flank.

61 Seán MacBride (1904–88), Stuart's brother-in-law, son of Major John MacBride, executed 1916 leader, and half-brother of Iseult Gonne.

62 Richard Mulcahy (1886–1971) GOC of National Army, Minister for Defence and TD for Dublin North-West. His wife Josephine was a sister of Dr James Ryan who was Campbell's cell-mate for a time in Mountjoy.

63 Norah Howell, an English woman and relative of his wife with whom Campbell seems to have been conducting an affair by correspondence. See the reference in the entry of 10 June to his being 'in trouble over a woman'.

64 Niall Plunkett Boyle, also known as Seán Plunkett, led a guerilla group in South Dublin and Wicklow in the early months of 1923. He was killed in an action near Valleymount, Co. Wicklow on 15 May.

65 General Seán MacEoin (1893–1973), commander of the Midland Division of National Army. Known as 'the Blacksmith of Ballinalee' for his defence of that village against British forces during the War of Independence in February 1921.

66 Patrick Mulrennan was shot dead by Commandant-General Lawlor during a riot in Athlone jail on 6 October 1922.

67 The world championship boxing match between Battling Siki and McTigue took place in Dublin on 17 March 1923.

68 Mary MacSwiney (*c.*1872–1942) Republican activist, sister of Terence MacSwiney (1879–1920), Lord Mayor of Cork who died on hunger-strike in Brixton Prison in October 1920. She attempted to raise Irish-American funds to support the Republican cause.

69 Alberta V. Montgomery, of Greyabbey, Co.Down, corresponded with Campbell during his imprisonment. She was possibly '*E[ithne] na M[ainistreach]*' ['Eithne of the Abbey'] to whom he dedicated *The Man-Child* in 1907. She reviewed the book in *Planet* the same year. Campbell's next collection, *The Gilly of Christ*, was dedicated to 'A.V.M.'

70 Unidentified, presumably a civilian worker in the camp. Referred to elsewhere as the 'shit-house man', he carried letters for Seán Kavanagh.

71 'Three Graces' is a reference to Maud Gonne MacBride (1866–1953), her friend Mrs Charlotte Despard (1884–1939), a suffragist and sister of Viscount French, Lord Lieutenant of Ireland 1918–21, and Iseult Gonne, Stuart's wife. They frequently appeared together at Republican demonstrations.
72 Widow of Cathal Brugha (1874–1922), Republican leader who had died of wounds on 7 July 1922, she was a member of a Sinn Féin committee set up in June 1923 to reorganise the Republican movement.
73 Robert Lambert, IRA leader in Wexford.
74 Adjutant, Dingle battalion.
75 Nickname of a soldier who conveyed letters in and out for Kavanagh.
76 Timothy Healy (1855–1931), former Nationalist MP; opponent of Parnell in the 1890s who became a supporter of the movement for independence after 1916. Appointed first Governor-General of Free State in 1922.
77 The Labour Party objected to the ceremonial of allegiance to the British Crown imposed by the Anglo-Irish Treaty. See Gaughan, *Thomas Johnson*, pp. 213–14.
78 John Dillon (1851–1927), leader of the major anti-Parnellite section of the Irish Parliamentary Party, 1891–1900, and leader of the remnant of the reunited party again in 1918–19. He had instigated the 'Plan of Campaign' (see note 23 above) with William O'Brien (1852–1928), another Irish Party MP.
79 Desmond FitzGerald (see note 16).
80 North Dublin Union Workhouse was used as a women's prison.
81 A rumour of his son's death in action had come into the camp on 28th September. It turned out later to be false.
82 The O'Rahilly, founder-member of Volunteers, killed 1916.
83 David Fitzpatrick informs me that this popular song was also the theme song of the 1932 rioters in Belfast.
84 Area in south Co. Dublin.
85 Medieval Irish mock-heroic text largely preoccupied with food and eating.
86 Hugh Boyle Kennedy (1879–1936), Attorney-General of the Free State, 1922–4.
87 Ernest Blythe (1889–1975), early member of Irish Volunteers, TD for North Monaghan, Minister for Local Government.
88 The rumour was untrue; in any case he was in fact in Kilmainham.
89 Brother of W. T. Cosgrave, President of Executive Council. Governor of Mountjoy.
90 Intelligence Officer.
91 Francis Sheehy-Skeffington (1878–1916), a pacifist and feminist, shot by the British, while a prisoner in Portobello Barracks, during the 1916 Rising. Sir John Simon presided over a Royal Commission of enquiry into the shooting.
92 Terence MacSwiney's funeral was not allowed to pass through Dublin by the authorities, and a day of mourning was held instead.

93 See notes above for O'Malley, Stack, Kilroy, Gallagher and David Robinson. George Plunkett was a younger brother of Joseph Plunkett, shot in 1916.

94 Mary MacSwiney spent 25 days on hunger-strike in Kilmainham Jail (1923).

95 Widow of The O'Rahilly.

96 The election was won by Hugh Kennedy of Cumann na nGaedheal.

97 The discovery of the tunnel.

98 May be Gerard Myles of Tralee who had fought in Kerry and Tipperary.

99 TD, prominent in War of Independence.

100 He had died on hunger-strike on 20 November.

101 Also known as Tomás Mac Cathmhaoil. A solicitor, he had organised Republican courts in Mayo during the War of Independence.

102 Strongbow (Richard de Clare), first invader of Ireland on behalf of King Henry II. Sir Felim O'Neill: leader of the 1641 rising in Ulster. Rinuccini: Papal nuncio to the Confederation of Kilkenny in the 1640s. Owen Roe (Eoghan Rua) O'Neill (?1584–1649) General of Irish forces of Confederation in 1640s. Patrick Sarsfield, Earl of Lucan (d. 1693), led Irish forces against Williamite armies in 1690s.

103 Name of a girl in Kilmallock, Co. Limerick, correspondent of Kavanagh.

104 Tomás Derrig was Adjutant General and Director of Intelligence of anti-Treaty forces until captured in April 1923. Séumas Robinson had led anti-Treaty forces in Tipperary. 'Seumas' here is a mistake for David L. Robinson, jail adjutant in Kilmainham. Dorothy Macardle says that Derrig and Robinson 'were escorted, still fasting, although they had been forty-one days without food on a tour of the camps and jails' to call off the strike; Macardle, *Irish Republic,* p. 790.

105 Kevin O'Higgins (1892–1927), TD for South Dublin and Minister for Justice.

106 Badge worn by Irish speakers.

107 Carrie Townshend was married to Bernard Shaw. Nancy Campbell had written to Shaw asking for help in bringing about Campbell's release. Her friend Mabel FitzGerald, wife of Desmond FitzGerald, ex-Minister for External Affairs (see note 16) had been Shaw's secretary. W. B. Yeats had presumably been approached as a member of the Senate. Æ was the pseudonym of George Russell (1867–1935), writer and mystic and editor of the *Irish Statesman.*

108 Denis Lacey, IRA leader in Tipperary, was shot dead in the Glen of Aherlow in February 1923.

109 John Weldon (1890–1963) whose pseudonym was Brinsley MacNamara, published a novel, *The Valley of the Squinting Windows* (1918), which led to litigation and a boycott of his father's school in Delvin, Co Westmeath.

110 Edward Plunkett, 18th Baron Dunsany (1878–1957), author of mythological stories and plays, lived at Dunsany, Co. Meath.

111 The poet Francis Ledwidge (1891–1917), killed in the First World War, was encouraged by Dunsany.

112 Sir Horace Plunkett (1854–1932), pioneer of the Irish agricultural cooperative movement and a Free State Senator, was an uncle of Dunsany's. His house, Kilteragh in Foxrock, was burned by the IRA.

113 Cardinal Logue, Archbishop of Armagh (1840–1924), had appealed for an end to the hunger-strike and the release of all prisoners not guilty of crimes.

Bibliography

Andrews, C.S., *Dublin Made Me: An Autobiography* (Dublin, 1979)

Campbell, Joseph, *Poems* (ed. with an introduction by Austin Clarke, Dublin, 1963)

Coogan, Tim Pat, *De Valera: Long Fellow, Long Shadow* (London, 1993)

FitzGerald, Fergus, ed., *Memoirs of Desmond FitzGerald, 1913–1916* (London, 1968)

Gallagher, Frank, *Days of Fear* (Cork, 1967)

Gaughan, J. Anthony (ed.), *Memoirs of Senator Joseph Connolly* (Dublin,1996)

Gaughan, J. Anthony, *Thomas Johnson, 1872–1963, First Leader of the Labour Party in Dáil Éireann* (Dublin, 1980)

Hopkinson, Michael, *Green Against Green: The Irish Civil War* (Dublin, 1988)

Jordan, Anthony J., *Seán MacBride: A Biography* (Dublin, 1993)

Macardle, Dorothy, *The Irish Republic* (London, [1937] 1968)

O'Donnell, Peadar, *The Gates Flew Open* (London, 1932)

O'Farrell, Padraic, *Who's Who in the Irish War of Independence and Civil War, 1916–1923* (Dublin, 1997)

O'Malley, Ernie, *The Singing Flame* (Dublin, 1978)

Saunders, Sr. Assumpta (ed.), *Journal of Irish Literature*, VIII, 3, September 1979 (Joseph Campbell special issue)

Saunders, Norah and Kelly, A.A., *Joseph Campbell: Poet and Nationalist 1879–1944* (Dublin, 1988)

Stuart, Francis, *Black List, Section H* (London, 1975)

Index